WHAT TO DO AFTER AN ACCIDENT

a Consumer Publication

edited by   Edith Rudinger

published by   Consumers' Association
publishers of **Which?**

illustrations by   Jo Bampton

Which? Books are commissioned and researched
by The Association for Consumer Research
and published by Consumers' Association,
14 Buckingham Street, London WC2N 6DS and
Hodder and Stoughton, 47 Bedford Square,
London WC1B 3DF

© Consumers' Association Ltd
March 1987

ISBN 0 340 39597 4
and   0 85202 327 8

Photoset by Paston Press, Loddon, Norfolk
Printed by Page Bros. (Norwich) Ltd.

WHAT TO DO
AFTER AN ACCIDENT

a Consumer Publication

Consumers' Association
publishers of **Which?**
14 Buckingham Street
London WC2N 6DS

CONTENTS

FOREWORD

This is a book to be read now, before an accident happens to you. Then read it again immediately after one, and refer to it while pursuing a claim for compensation or applying for payments because of injuries or damage arising from the accident.

The book does not attempt to give instructions on first aid that should be administered at the time. There are many specialist books and pamphlets describing emergency first aid procedures, and courses that can be taken to teach what should and should not be done to an injured person.

Injury due to professional negligence is outside the scope of the book. This is a different category of 'accident' with even more complex procedures and long-drawn-out negotiations.

Accidents occurring outside the UK and multiple accidents (for instance, a motorway pile-up or air crash) are not covered, nor does the book deal with the situation when the victim dies as a result of the accident.

An accident can have a devastating effect. You should try to avoid having or causing an accident by being careful and considerate when at home, in the street, in a shop, at work, driving, getting on and off trains and buses, walking or cycling, to ensure that you never need to use this book.

Throughout this book

for 'he' read 'he or she'

INTRODUCTION

No one normally goes out every day prepared for an accident to happen, with pen or pencil and notebook, tape measure, camera, recording machine, details of insurance ready to hand. The action that should be taken immediately after an accident presupposes a cool and rational state of mind. But when you have just been injured, you are likely to be in a state of shock and unable to go round taking notes and getting statements, and may well say things that you later regret. Knowing what ideally should be done – and what should not be done – can help to take the right action at the time in case a claim for compensation needs to be made later.

After you have been in an accident, you will be disorientated to some degree and will need to direct your energies to coping with pain and disablement and immediate practical matters concerning family and job. But you must be prepared to talk sensibly about the accident to a solicitor and to deal with the questions he will ask, and to go through documents and fill in applications and report forms that insurance companies and government departments may require.

However depressed you may feel at times in the face of delays, bureaucracy, and an avalanche of forms, documents and statements, do not give up. If you are aware of what ought to happen, you should be able to avoid being misled by inefficiency or incompetence or frustrated by delaying tactics or defeated by people who try to fob you off.

Do not attempt a do-it-yourself job on a personal injury claim. You will need the advice of a solicitor with the appropriate experience and it will be helpful to know something about what he should be doing on your behalf by taking action along the lines described in this book.

what you can get

Much of this book is concerned with claims under the law of negligence. But in many cases, legal compensation for negligence is a less important means of providing for the victim of an accident than payments from the state and payments from employers and insurance policies.

An accident can be expensive. Even a minor one can put you out of action so that you lose pay or earnings as well as giving rise to extra expenses. After a serious accident, you will not only have to contend with pain and injury, but you may have to pay for special equipment, adaptations to the home and extra household care. And you may find that your future earning potential is reduced.

There are a number of different ways in which you can claim for the financial consequences of an accident, from different sources each with its own criteria. You should find out about and claim whatever you are due in the circumstances. There is no reason why you should not claim on all available sources, where appropriate, although getting payment from one may affect the payment from another.

benefits from the state

You and your family may be entitled to one or more of numerous social security benefits.

Means-tested benefits, such as supplementary benefit and housing benefit are designed to meet minimum living expenses; statutory sick pay, sickness benefit and invalidity benefits are designed to compensate for lost earnings; benefits for the severely disabled, such as mobility allowance, attendance allowance and severe disablement allowance help with the costs of long-term disability. In addition, invalid care alowance can be paid to someone who cares for a disabled person full-time. If you suffer an accident at work, special 'industrial' social security benefits are available, at higher rates than standard benefits.

These can all be claimed, as of right, through the DHSS.

benefits for employees

The majority of employees are entitled to some pay when they are off work because of an injury, for the first three months or perhaps up to six months. Employers set their own terms and conditions for paying employees who are off sick.

Someone who is a member of an occupational pension scheme may be entitled to retire early on a reduced pension due to ill health. Generally, the longer you have been with the employer, the more you will get.

A small number of employers arrange for 'permanent health' insurance on a group basis for their employees, so that payment comes from an insurance company for as long as the employee is unable to work.

personal insurance

Someone who has taken out personal accident insurance or has 'permanent health' insurance can claim on that for payments during the period of recovery, according to the terms of the particular policy.

compensation through the law

In addition to the payments which can be claimed by an injured person irrespective of how the accident was caused and regardless of whose fault it was, if you can prove that your accident was someone else's fault and that his or her negligence has damaged you or your property, you will be able to claim compensation from that person under the law. Whether you actually get any payment will depend on the other person being able to pay (either out of his or her own resources or because of being insured for such liability).

The initiative for making and proving a negligence claim lies with you, the victim. You should take legal advice initially, and will probably need legal and other professional help with pursuing a claim. You may have to threaten, and even take, court proceedings. The vast majority of cases, however, are eventually resolved by out-of-court negotiations between the lawyers on both sides.

In response to the Lord Chancellor's review of personal injury litigation in England and Wales, the National Consumer Council commented in 1986 that "around a tenth of the 3 million people injured each year engage in a difficult, long-winded and expensive battle with an insurance company. How they fare will depend more on their knowledge and stamina and on the skills of their lawyers than on . . . the severity of the injuries or the degree of blameworthiness. Most people do not get any compensation because they do not know their rights or do not know how to exercise them. Those who do receive payment have experienced long delays and considerable anxiety."

ACTION AT THE SCENE OF AN ACCIDENT

If you are with somebody involved in an accident, or come across an accident in which someone has been injured, your action may save a life. Your initial response may be one of panic or a lack of confidence but there are some actions you should take.

calling for help

Ensure that a competent person telephones for the emergency services using the '999' system. Any of the services will inform the others: ambulance will call police and fire if required, depending on the information given.

When dialling '999', you will be asked for the number from which you are calling. This is not in order that a charge may be made but to ensure that, should you be cut off for any reason, your location will be obtainable via the operator.

State clearly what has happened, how many people are injured and whether any of them appear to be trapped.

Give as exact a location of the incident as you can. ". . . . outside Boots in the High Street" is not sufficient. They will need to know which High Street and the number, if possible. It is helpful if you are able to refer to a local landmark such as church or pub.

first aid

Injured people should be left where they are, unless there is a risk of fire.

While waiting for the ambulance to arrive, do not attempt to carry out more than basic first aid unless you know what you are doing.

○ ensure that the airway is clear and that the person can breathe
○ if the airway is clear but the person is not breathing, start mouth-to-mouth resuscitation
○ if the person is bleeding, control the bleeding by placing a pad over the area and pressing firmly.

Anyone who is involved in an accident will be in shock. Treat the shock by reassuring the patient and keeping him or her warm. Do not overheat them and give nothing to drink.

waiting for the ambulance
Try to note the circumstances of the accident, how it happened, who else was involved or witnessed it.

When the ambulance arrives, get someone to meet it or wave it down.

in the ambulance
The ambulance crew normally take a relative or friend to the hospital with the victim. Sometimes, however, this may not be possible, especially if there are two patients who require stretchers. Should this be the case, ask which hospital the patient will be taken to. Do not assume you know; the crew may need to convey the patient to a specialist unit, or the local hospital casualty department may be closed for one reason or another.

If you go with the injured person in the ambulance, you should remain seated, for your own safety. The crew will be occupied in attending to the patient, who is obviously their main priority.

If you are not able to travel in the ambulance and are unable to make your own way, the police, who will normally be present at the scene, may be able to assist you.

arriving at the hospital

When you arrive at the hospital, you will usually be asked to wait in the area provided, while the hospital staff are taking over from the ambulance crew and settling the patient into a cubicle.

During this time, you may be able to assist by giving the receptionist the patient's particulars, and any other medical information you are able to provide.

informing the relatives

It is best not to inform relatives until the doctor who is treating the patient has informed you of his or her condition.

In cases of serious or fatal injury, this task may be better left to the police, who are experienced in these matters.

WHEN YOU ARE INJURED

If you are badly hurt, someone should have sent for an ambulance and may have called the police. In some circumstances, the police will notify your family or friends or employer. Try to ask whoever is with you, or comes to help you, to note what had happened and who was there and any special circumstances.

at hospital

When you arrive at hospital after an accident, there may be very little information about you available for the hospital staff – perhaps not even your name. Ideally, everyone should always carry some means of identification: name, address, telephone number, details of next of kin or person to contact. Additional helpful information would be blood group, note of any allergies (for example, to penicillin), a hospital number.

minor injuries

If your injury is of a minor nature, you will be given treatment in the accident and emergency unit (casualty department) and will then be referred to the care of your general practitioner.

Try to remember what was done at the hospital in the way of treatment of your injury (and, for example, whether X-rays were taken) and what you were told to do and not to do. If you were confused after the accident and when you return home cannot remember what the hospital staff told you, you can telephone the hospital later and ask to speak to the nurse-in-charge of the accident and emergency unit. Give your name, and the date and time you were at the hospital, and he or she will be able to tell you what had been done.

Arrange to see your GP as soon as you can so that he can note the initial state of your injury and treatment.

An appointment may be made for you at the hospital to come back to see a doctor in the outpatient department. You will be given an appointment card listing the date and time of the appointment, the consultant responsible for your treatment, and your hospital registration number. Or your GP may arrange this after he has seen the extent or development of your injury.

Make it clear to the doctor (GP or hospital) that if your injury looks like being serious in its effects, you may want to claim compensation from whoever caused the accident. The doctor can then make his notes at the time with the awareness that he may later be asked to prepare a formal report about your condition to be used as evidence in a claim for damages.

being an inpatient

If your injuries are so bad that you need more care than the emergency treatment that can be given at the casualty department, you will be admitted as an inpatient and sent up to one of the wards. The staff there will ask for more detailed information, if you are in a fit state to give this, about your circumstances and background.

If you have any valuables with you (watch, money, rings and suchlike), the nurse-in-charge on the ward may take them for safe keeping (and will give you a receipt) until you can arrange for them to be taken home.

You will be in the care of a consultant who decides about your treatment and who will make periodic visits to check how you are getting on. Your day-to-day care will be undertaken by his registrar and other medical personnel and nurses on the ward, and in other departments (X-ray, pathology, physiotherapy and so on).

If you or your family would like information about your injury or condition, ask the nurse-in-charge or the daily doctor who attends you. You can ask the consultant, too, on his rarer appearances; relatives would have to make a specific appointment, through the nurse-in-charge, if they want to discuss your condition and prognosis (forecast of what to expect).

specialist services

When the initial, perhaps life-saving, measures have been taken after an accident, you may be referred for specialist treatment.

There are special NHS hospitals and units, some providing a district service and others serving a region or covering several regions (the national health service is divided into regions and sub-divided into districts). Private treatment by a particular consultant or hospital is an option.

You do not have to be treated in the health authority region in which you live if there are more appropriate facilities elsewhere. The hospital doctor can refer you to a suitable specialist unit.

Specialist orthopaedic hospitals or units provide special expertise for more complicated fractures or where a fracture will not unite, and for peripheral nerve lesions; may have a doctor with particular interest in back problems.

Hand surgeons are orthopaedic or plastic surgeons who have specialised in the treatment of hand injuries and are skilled in carrying out the intricate surgery of the hand; may be based in the local district general hospital or be practising in another hospital within the district or region.

Plastic surgeons have particular skills in reconstructing and repairing the surface of the body – for example, after burns; understand how to minimise scarring and distortion of facial contours.

Regional burns units specialise in treating people with severe burns, using techniques to reduce scarring and minimise deformity.

Head injury and spinal injury units (of which there are only few) provide specialist rehabilitation after a head or spinal injury (perhaps the most devastating disabilities that can follow an accident).

personal affairs

If you are worried about your family, home, job or finances, the nurse-in-charge can contact the hospital social work department and get a social worker to come to discuss your problems. There are numerous services and allowances available to help you cope with temporary or permanent disability. Relatives also can contact the social work department at the hospital direct to get advice on what can be done to help you.

Claim forms and medical certificates for claiming state benefits can be provided by the nurse-in-charge. It is important that you keep on submitting medical certificates to your employer or the social security office for the whole of your stay in hospital.

If you have to stay in hospital for any length of time when you are getting certain social security payments (such as supplementary benefit, sickness benefit, retirement pension), the payment will be reduced or stopped. You are meant to notify the social security office as soon as possible after you have become an inpatient so that they can check and adjust your entitlement to benefit. (DHSS leaflet NI.9 explains what happens to your social security benefit or pension on going into hospital.) You can ask the nurse-in-charge to do this if you have no one to do so for you. Also, she can be asked to arrange for your weekly orders for a benefit payment to be cashed for you while you are in hospital.

preparing for your claim

With a major injury when you are removed immediately to hospital, you will have been unable to take the necessary action of making notes at the scene. But, even while confined to bed, you should ask a friend or relative to do as much as possible about gathering evidence, obtaining witnesses and taking other appropriate action straight away.

If it is not convenient for your solicitor to come to see you during normal hospital visiting hours, ask the nurse-in-charge whether the solicitor can come at another mutually convenient time. There is not much privacy for conversation in a ward, even with the curtains drawn around the bed, but when you are able to get out of bed, you may be able to arrange to have an interview in a separate room or office.

Any information concerning your medical condition is strictly confidential and will not be given to anyone other than your GP without your permission. So, if your solicitor needs information about the extent of your injury or your treatment, he will have to make his request through you or with your formal authorisation.

discharge from hospital

As soon as the doctors consider you fit to leave hospital, the nurse-in-charge will make arrangements for you to go home or to an appropriate convalescent or rehabilitation establishment. The ward clerk will want to have your home address in case any mail has to be forwarded.

If you need transport, an ambulance will be arranged to take you home. Otherwise, you are responsible for your own journey home. A relative or friend who comes for you should bring clothes for you to go home in, plus a case or bag for the belongings you have with you in the hospital.

Any home nursing services you require will be booked for you. It may be thought necessary for the occupational therapist to visit your home beforehand to assess any potential problems there, if your injury has left your mobility impaired in any way.

Ask about the procedure for the return or replacement of any aids or equipment supplied by the hospital, such as calipers, or a walking frame or stick.

You may be given tablets or medicine to take at home. Make sure you understand the instructions for taking these; check the name of the drug and what you should do if you need a further supply.

If you are likely to be needing medication for some time to come, and you do not qualify for free NHS prescriptions, you can save money by buying a 'season ticket' in the form of a prepayment certificate. For £12, you can get a certificate to cover four months; for £33.50, a certificate to cover up to a year. DHSS leaflet P.11 gives details of who qualifies for free prescriptions and what proof is required and explains about prepayment certificates and where to get form FP.95 (in Scotland, EC.95) on which to apply.

further treatment
After your discharge, a letter will be sent by the hospital doctor to your GP, with information about your treatment and any after-care needed. Thereafter, you return to the care of your GP, and any treatment or nursing services you require will be arranged through him.

You may have an appointment booked for you at the hospital for follow-up treatment as an outpatient. If so, you will be given a card with the date and time, and doctor's name. If you were in hospital a long way from home, that hospital can arrange for any follow-up outpatient treatment to be transferred to a consultant at your local hospital.

Make sure that you cooperate fully with any treatment recommended, and attend all hospital appointments for checkup. If there is good reason not to attend, put it in writing when you cancel the appointment.

If the cost of getting to or from hospital for outpatient appointments is a hardship to you, you may qualify for help with fares. DHSS leaflet H.11 explains what travel costs can be refunded and who can claim. You claim the refund at the hospital each time you visit (it will be sent to you by post if you are not going back to the hospital). If you need the money in advance to pay your fare in order to get to hospital, you should ask your local social security office.

PAYMENT FROM THE STATE

If your injury prevents you from working, you can claim payments from the state social security system, through the Department of Health and Social Security (DHSS). Many of these 'benefits' depend on having paid national insurance contributions while working during previous years. If the injury occurred directly as a result of employment, however, a benefit may also be payable under the industrial injuries scheme, for which there are no contribution requirements.

employees and statutory sick pay

Your employer must pay you statutory sick pay (SSP) once you have been away for more than 4 days. The prescribed weekly rate depends on your average weekly earnings. The SSP rates are revised each year in April; the 1987 figures are:

£32.85 if your pay is between £39 and £76.49 a week

£47.20 if your pay is £76.50 or more a week.

Anyone earning less than £39 a week (the 1987/88 threshold for paying national insurance contributions) does not get SSP but can apply for sickness benefit direct from the DHSS.

There is no need to claim SSP specifically, but when you are ill for more than 4 days in a row (including weekends and non-working days), you must notify your employer of your incapacity according to the rules he has laid down. Each employer can stipulate his own requirements about the timing and method of notification and about any evidence you should provide.

The employer has to pay you SSP for any 'qualifying' days (other than the first three) you are away from work. These are usually the days for which you are contracted to work. So, if you normally work for only 3 days a week, you do not get SSP for the other 2 weekdays.

Statutory sick pay is treated as if it were salary, so any tax and national insurance contributions will be deducted from it. If, however, you are only paid SSP at the lower rate (currently £32.85), this will be below the level on which you have to pay national insurance contributions, and these can be credited to you instead if this is found to be necessary at the end of the year to keep up your contribution record.

The maximum period for which an employer has to pay SSP is 28 weeks. This period can extend over 3 years provided that the gap between bouts of being off work is never more than 8 weeks, and can be carried forward from a previous employer. This means that if your injury fluctuates in its effect, so that you are able to go back to work for a few weeks but then it flares up and keeps you at home, you do not have the three 'waiting' days again before getting SSP.

If you are well enough to return to work for more than 8 full weeks, your SSP standing goes back to the start, so that, if you are then unable to work again, you get another maximum period of 28 weeks (less 3 'waiting' days).

Once you have exhausted your 28-week entitlement to SSP and you are still incapacitated, you can transfer to the state invalidity benefit (provided that you would have satisfied the contribution conditions for receiving sickness benefit). A few weeks before this would become necessary, your employer should let you have a transfer form, SSP 1(T), incorporating a claim for invalidity benefit. This has to be sent to the local social security office in time for the changeover to be made after the 28th week if you are still unable to work then.

Leaflet NI 227 is the employer's guide to statutory sick pay and contains details of what the employer has to do at the different stages of an employee's illness. For employees, leaflet NI 244 tells you how to check your right to statutory sick pay, and leaflets NI 208 and NI 196 include current SSP rates of payment.

SSP is a minimum. Some employers have their own sick pay scheme which may be more generous in its criteria, length of payment and amount.

non-employees and sickness benefit

Someone whose injury prevents him or her from working and
who is
- wholly self-employed, or
- over state pension age, or
- unemployed, or
- employed but earning less than the lower earnings limit for
  paying national insurance contributions, or
- employed but taken on for a specific period of not more than
  3 months, or
- on strike, or
- employed but has not yet actually started work

does not qualify for statutory sick pay but can claim the state
sickness benefit through the DHSS.

Being paid sickness benefit depends on the number of
national insurance contributions made during the tax year
ending before the calendar year in which benefit is claimed.
Leaflet NI 16 deals in detail with sickness benefit and qualifications and claims, and NI 196 gives the current rates of payment
and the increases for dependants.

To claim sickness benefit, fill in form SC1, available at social
security offices, doctors' surgeries and hospitals. This is a
self-certification form, treated as evidence of illness for the first
week. After 7 days off work, you will need a doctor's sick-note
as evidence of your continuing incapacity. The doctor must
provide this free of charge. The doctor will give you either a
'closed' note saying on which date he thinks you can go back to
work or an 'open' note, which means you have to go back to
see him again for another note on the date he has specified. Be
sure to go to see the doctor again then – you may lose out on
sickness benefit if you do not go and there is a gap not covered
by a doctor's note. Complete and send the doctor's note
straight away to the social security office each time he gives
you one.

It is important not to delay in claiming sickness benefit

because payment is not normally backdated beyond set limits from the date a claim is made. The limits are

1 month if a first-ever claim

6 days (not including sunday) if the first claim in a spell of sickness

10 days (not including sundays) if a continuation claim.

You may be – but should not rely on being – allowed to get your payment backdated further; if you are sending your form in late, enclose a letter explaining the reasons for the delay. For instance, if you have been in hospital as an inpatient, more time will be given.

The amount of sickness benefit is (for 1987/88)

£37.85 a week if you are over pension age

£30.05 a week for anyone else.

This will be increased for a spouse whom you live with or are maintaining (unless he or she is earning more than the amount of the increase) or for an adult dependant. There are other increases for some other dependants in specified circumstances. You should tick on form SC1 that you want to claim for dependants and you will be sent another form on which to give information about them.

After your initial claim, you will in due course (it should not be more than 14 days) be told how much benefit it has been decided to pay you (or none at all). With this notification, you will be sent information about how to appeal if you do not agree with the proposed payment or non-payment.

Sickness benefit does not start until the fourth day of illness and is paid for a maximum of 28 weeks. It is not taxable.

People under state pension are age credited with national insurance contributions while they are receiving sickness benefit (or are submitting sick-notes even if not being paid benefit) so their national insurance record is kept going without a break, and a future pension or other contribution-based benefit is not affected.

When you have been receiving sickness benefit for a total of

28 weeks and are still incapable of work, you will receive invalidity benefit, which is paid at a higher rate than sickness benefit.

long-term invalidity benefit

If, after the maximum period for getting SSP (which works out as 168 days in total, excluding sundays), you are still incapacitated from working, you may be eligible for invalidity benefit. You should claim invalidity benefit on form SSP1(T) supplied by your employer. A claim should be made earlier than the 28th week (even if it is not clear whether incapacity will continue) to enable the contribution records to be checked – a matter of about 2 weeks.

Anyone who has been receiving sickness benefit should be transferred automatically when sickness benefit ends, or can make a claim on form SC1(Rev), available at a hospital, doctor's surgery, social security office.

The basic payment you get is called invalidity pension. Added to this, you may be entitled to

○ an earnings-related addition
This additional component may be paid to an employed person, based on earnings since April 1978 on which class 1 national insurance contributions have been paid.
○ an allowance related to your age
Someone who was under the age of 60 (man) or 55 (woman) on the first day when the injury prevented work may get an invalidity allowance as well as the basic invalidity pension. The allowance is higher the younger you were at the start, and decreases in decades: under 40 the highest rate, between 40 and 49 the middle rate, between 50 and 59 (men) or 54 (women) the lowest rate. If eligible for an additional earnings-related payment, the invalidity allowance is reduced by the amount of the earnings-related component.
○ increases for dependants
An increase to the basic invalidity pension will be paid for

one adult dependant (spouse or other adult looking after your children) and for dependent children, subject to earnings limits.

You will have to go on sending sick-notes from your doctor to the social security office for as long as your disability prevents you from working.

Invalidity benefit is not taxable, and while you are receiving it, you will be credited with national insurance contributions, up to state retirement age.

If your national insurance contributions would entitle you to a reduced retirement pension, after retirement age your invalidity pension will be proportionately reduced (but not the age allowance component).

Leaflet NI 16A explains invalidity benefit in detail, and leaflet NI 196 gives the current rates.

severe disablement allowance

Someone under state pension age whose national insurance record does not qualify him or her for sickness benefit or invalidity benefit can claim severe disablement allowance – but only after 28 weeks of being incapable of work because of injury. This payment is at a lower rate than sickness benefit or invalidity benefit would be, and usually depends on the assessed degree of disability being at least 80 per cent. The allowance is tax-free. Increases are payable for children and for a spouse or an adult who is looking after your children. Leaflet NI 252 gives details and contains a comprehensive claim form (SDA 1).

sources of help and information

The Child Poverty Action Group's *Rights guide to non-means-tested social security benefits* (1987 edition £4.50) includes full details, advice and information on all these state benefits. The CPAG's address is 1–5 Bath Street, London EC1V 9PY.

Non-means-tested benefits provide a very modest level of income. If this is insufficient for your needs, you may be able to claim means-tested extra allowance and benefits (such as supplementary benefit). The CPAG's *National welfare benefits handbook* deals with these.

For general information and advice on financial help from the state, dial 100 and ask the operator for 'Freefone DHSS'.

PAYMENT FROM AN INSURANCE POLICY

Anyone with 'personal accident' insurance can apply to the insurers for payment due under the terms of the policy. The insurance may be a separate personal accident policy or in a section of another policy, such as household or holiday, or from a group policy such as a sports club's.

Anyone with 'permanent health' insurance whose disability is long-term and affects the capacity to earn can claim on this insurance.

There are also 'hospital cash' policies which pay out a sum for a set number of days while you are in hospital; some personal accident policies include such payments, too.

Such insurances are not mutually exclusive and the payments are not reduced because of any other payments you are receiving or are awarded: you get the specified amount due for the premiums you have been paying, provided the policy conditions are fulfilled. There will, however, be a limit under a permanent health insurance policy on the total you can receive per week.

Claims under personal insurance policies are not dependent on proving someone else's fault or negligence.

personal accident insurance

Look carefully at the terms of the policy to discover what injuries are covered and how and by when you should claim.

There are some circumstances which are excluded from these policies: accidents occurring while undertaking certain hazardous activities or when wilfully exposing yourself to danger unnecessarily; disablement or injury contributed to by pre-existent health defects; accidents occurring while under the influence of drink or drugs. That apart, you will be able to claim on the policy even if an injury is the result of an accident caused by a careless or unfortunate act of your own.

You cannot claim if the accident occurs within a specified number of weeks after the policy was issued (the waiting period).

Tell the insurers as soon as reasonably possible of any circumstances that may give rise to a claim. The results of some injuries take time to show their full effects. Even if in doubt about whether an injury is going to be serious enough to merit a claim, notify the insurers and ask for a claim form. There will be a stipulated period (1 year or 2 years usually) from the accident within which the claim must be made.

claiming
The claim form which the insurers will send you requires certain information about the accident, about the conse-quences of the accident, about you and your current occupa-tion. Before meeting a claim, the insurers may want to find out whether you really are totally unable to work.

Typical questions on an accident claim form would be

what were you doing when the accident happened?
This is to find out whether you were doing anything particu-larly hazardous or any activity excluded by the policy, such as racing.

names and addresses of witnesses
Witnesses may help you prove that your injury was due to a genuine accident. Tell them that you are giving their names to your insurers.

what is the extent of your injuries?
This allows the insurers to assess whether it is reasonable that these injuries resulted solely from the accident as described

and allows them to estimate the claim. Even if the injuries are relatively minor, if you have consulted your GP or been treated at a hospital casualty department, there will be a record of the injury and/or treatment.

when did disability start?
This is not necessarily when the accident happened (you may not have had to stop work immediately), but the date when you became unable to work.

what you get
What you may get is a weekly payment for a set number of weeks (maximum 104) while you are unable to do your job and a lump sum if the injury leaves you totally and permanently disabled or with the loss of an eye or ear or a limb. Certain policies make only a lump payment, not interim weekly payments.

By having paid a slightly higher premium, you may get a lump sum payment on the 'continental scale'. This means that a specified percentage of the sum insured is paid for loss or loss of use of different parts of the body. For example:

loss by amputation or permanent total loss of use of
one or more limbs 100%
one big toe 10%
any other toe 5%
one thumb 25% right, 20% left
one forefinger 20% right, 6% left
(The 'right' and 'left' percentages are reversed if the person is left handed.)

With a policy not on the continental scale you might get, for example, 100% of the lump sum if you had your hand amputated, but nothing for the loss of your thumb. A policy on the continental scale would pay 25% for such a partial disability.

You can never get more than 100% in total for injuries resulting from one accident. If you lose the use of one arm and also two fingers from the other hand, you get only the one lump sum, not the extra percentage for the lost fingers.

If your policy covers 'loss' rather than 'loss of use', you will not get any payment unless the part (thumb, toe, ear or whatever) has had to be amputated. A better policy will cover loss of sight or loss of hearing, rather than physical loss of eye or ear.

Unless you have a policy which provides for temporary partial disablement, no weekly payment will be made once you return to work part-time.

Some policies also offer a small amount to pay for treatment and associated costs which arise directly from the injury ('medical expenses benefit') or a sum for each day or week you have to be in hospital as an inpatient after the first 24 hours.

cash while in hospital

A 'hospital cash plan' will pay a daily sum while you are in hospital following an accident, as an inpatient, for up to so-many days. These payments do not have to be applied towards hospital fees and are made even if treatment is given in an NHS hospital at no cost to you.

What you get would be nowhere near enough to pay for private treatment but could help to offset extra expenses, such as the cost of your family visiting you daily.

The hospital, NHS or private, must be one 'acceptable' under the terms of the policy – a geriatric or psychiatric hospital, for instance, is likely to be excluded. You have to obtain proof from the hospital that you were an inpatient for more than 24 hours. You may have to obtain a medical certificate from the hospital doctor. You may be asked to authorise the insurers to approach any doctor who has been treating you, to get further information on your condition.

If your stay in hospital is prolonged, an interim payment may be made; otherwise, a single payment is made after you have been discharged.

permanent health insurance

Anyone who has taken out 'permanent health' (PHI) or 're-placement income' insurance should already be aware of the restrictions and conditions of the particular policy and the deferment period (anything from 4 weeks to 104 weeks).

A deferment period means that for the first weeks when you are unable to work, the insurance will not pay you anything. For instance, if the deferment period is six weeks, you will be paid only from the 43rd day of disablement. If you go back to work after 40 days off, you will receive nothing. If you go back to work after seven weeks off, you will receive one week's-worth of benefit.

Normally, the insurers specify how long before the end of the deferment period you must notify them if you think your disablement is going to last longer.

A franchise, like a deferment period, cuts out claims for short periods of disablement. Unlike a deferment period, however, if the length of time off work is longer than the franchise period, you will be paid for every day off work right from the beginning.

claiming

You will be sent a claim form to complete which will ask for details of the injury.

There will be certain circumstances, specified in the policy, when you cannot claim payment – for example, if the disability was caused by a self-inflicted injury or by a riot or an act of war or insurrection, or through an accident when flying other than as a fare-paying passenger.

When the time is approaching for a payment to become due, you should prepare for your claim by assembling medical reports to prove that you qualify under the policy's definition of 'disablement': inability to do your own job or a similar job or any job.

The criterion is not how disabled you are, but whether you can go on earning a living. Your own doctor's report should be sufficient but in some cases the insurers may require an examination and report by their own medical man.

You will also need to produce evidence of your earnings during the 12 months preceding the accident.

payment
Once eligibility under the policy has been established, payments are made to you generally monthly in arrears, and will continue until you can resume work or until you reach normal retirement age. The insurers may require that you have periodic check-ups throughout the duration of your incapacity.

What you get will depend on the premium that you chose to pay and will be limited usually to 75 per cent of your total average earnings in the previous 12 months. Included in the calculations for this limit will be national insurance benefits and any other insurance payments (but income from personal accident policies lasting not more than 104 weeks is usually ignored), so that your income now cannot be more than 75 per cent of your previous earnings level. Some policies have different limits on payments and your permanent health policy may pay out far less than 75 per cent of your previous income.

If your disability continues for a long time, the insurers may ask your GP to estimate when a return to work can be anticipated.

Some insurers have established a disability counselling service, sending a counsellor (a nurse, generally) to visit long-term claimants.

Depending on the policy and the premium you had paid, there may be an automatic increase every year or so in the payments you receive.

The payment ceases if you are eventually able to return to your work full-time. If either you return to your old job on a part-time basis or you have to take up a less well-paid job full-time, the policy wil pay an amount to make up the difference. This is intended as an incentive to return to work as soon as it is reasonable to do so.

While you are getting payments, your premium to maintain the policy remains due, but will be waived if there is a 'benefit' under the policy conditions. Some policies include a 'waiver of premium benefit' for self-employed policyholders only.

tax

No income tax will be payable on the insurance payments until you have been receiving these for more than one complete tax year (6 April to 5 April). So, if your payments happened to start during the latter part of April one year, you would not be liable to pay tax on them until the tax year starting 6 April the year after the following one: they will be tax free for almost two years. In the second tax year and thereafter, the payments are liable to tax.

The exception to this can be if you have a personal accident policy and a permanent health insurance policy and the personal accident policy has a shorter deferred period than the permanent health insurance policy: the Inland Revenue tax 'clock' for the permanent health insurance policy starts running when the income under the personal accident policy becomes payable. Normally, a personal accident policy has a benefit payment period of too short a duration for the Revenue to bother about it, but they will take it into account in conjunction with the permanent health insurance policy to establish the existence of a regular income.

For a self-employed person, the payments received from a permanent health insurance policy are not treated as 'relevant earnings' by the Inland Revenue, and so cannot be used as the basis for making tax-relieved payments to a self-employed pension scheme.

insurance and claiming compensation

Neither permanent health insurance nor personal accident insurance is based on the principle of indemnity. You are not being compensated for what you have lost and any amounts you may receive under such cover do not have to be paid back to the insurers if you are successful in getting payment for damages from the person who caused the accident.

WHAT THE LAW SAYS

That part of the law under which a claim for damages after an accident is usually made is the law of tort (a mediaeval word meaning fault).

In order to pursue a successful claim for damages arising out of an accident, you must prove

○ that the person who caused the accident owed you a 'duty of care'
○ that there was a breach of that duty
○ that loss or injury resulted from this breach.

The tort of negligence embraces these three points.

Everybody owes a duty of care to their 'neighbour' and must ensure that they do not fail in that duty. In a classic case in 1932, Lord Atkin defined what came to be known as the 'neighbour principle' as follows:

> "The rule that you are to love your neighbour becomes in law that you must not injure your neighbour and the lawyer's question 'Who is my neighbour?' receives a restricted reply. You must take reasonable care to avoid acts or omissions which you can reasonably foresee would be likely to injure your neighbour. Who, then, in law is my neighbour? The answer seems to be persons who are so closely and directly affected by my act that I ought reasonably to have them in contemplation as being so affected when I am directing my mind to the acts or omissions which are called in question."

You must be able to show not only that the other person owed you a duty of care but also that he failed in that duty. Negligence has been classically defined as the "omission to do something which a reasonable man . . . would do, or doing something which a prudent and reasonable man would not do". What is and is not 'reasonable' will vary from case to case but generally the reasonable man is taken to be one who is no better and no worse than any other layman but who acts properly, exercising the same level of care as any reasonable person in these particular circumstances.

There must have been a loss: you can claim compensation only if you have actually suffered some injury or damage, whether physically, mentally, financially or otherwise. In some cases, this is easy to show. After a car accident, for example, the reasonable costs of repairs to a vehicle damaged in the accident clearly amount to a loss.

The courts' aim is to try and put the injured party as far as possible in the position in which he would have been if the accident had not taken place. That is not always possible. Whereas one can replace a broken window so that it is as good as new, one cannot remove pain caused by an injury. Under those circumstances, the law has to award a sum of money which will as near as possible compensate the injured party for the pain and trouble caused by the accident.

In court proceedings, the person bringing the claim is the plaintiff (in Scotland, pursuer) and the person or body being sued is the defendant (in Scotland, the defender).

liability

The basis of the common law is that a person should not be held liable for any incident unless it can be shown that he or she was responsible or in some way at fault. The defendant may be the person who actually injured you, or the person who has a vicarious liability – for example, where an employer is liable for the action of the employee, servant or agent.

There are exceptional cases, known as 'strict liability' cases, where you have to prove loss and that it was caused by the defendant, but you do not have to establish that the defendant was at fault in breach of duty of care. Strict liability arises mainly from duties laid down in certain statutes, such as the Factories Act 1961.

The law of contract may also be relevant in claiming damages. For instance, a landlord may be liable for damages arising from an accident caused by breach of an obligation to keep premises in repair; negligence would be irrelevant.

consent to risk

A claim for damages arising from an accident can only be made by someone who has not actually invited the damage by knowingly taking the risk of injury. The common law has built up the principle that a person has no claim if he has expressly or impliedly consented to intentional or accidental harm being inflicted on him. This principle is known as the 'volenti' rule, from the latin tag *volenti non fit injuria*.

The 'volenti' rule does not apply to rescuers who voluntarily expose themselves to danger by coming to the aid of someone in difficulties. It does apply, however, in a sport where there is a risk of injury by the nature of the sport (but does not extend to deliberate and malicious injury by the opponent).

contributory negligence

A defendant may oppose a claim, in all or in part, on the ground that the plaintiff failed to show proper care himself and that, had he shown that proper care, either the accident would not have happened or the damage involved would have been less. If it is shown that the defendant alone is not entirely responsible for the accident, or for the resulting loss, the amount of compensation awarded will be reduced by a percentage proportionate to the contributory negligence in the particular circumstances. This rule can even go to the extent of relieving a defendant of the requirement to pay any damages at all.

Contributory negligence is often found in road accidents, where one driver accepts that he was partly to blame for the accident but claims that the other driver contributed towards it by, for example, travelling too fast for the road conditions.

time limits

A claim for personal injuries must normally be brought within three years of the date when the injury was sustained. (For bringing a claim other than for personal injury, there are other limits.) In cases in which it is difficult to ascertain the precise date on which an injury was sustained, the time limit may start to run from the time when the injury was first reasonably discoverable.

It is important that you should get on with your claim as soon as you are aware of the injury, without waiting to see how far you recover, and that you start proceedings, if necessary, within the three-year limit. Proceedings are started when a writ or summons has been issued at the relevant court; if the writ or summons has not been served on the defendant straight away, this must be done within the next 12 months.

Delay in making or proceeding with a claim can lead to difficulties in gathering evidence and tracing witnesses, whose recollection of what happened may well become less reliable as the time goes by.

children
For a child, the limitation period of 3 years does not start to run until he reaches the age of 18. The 'child' then has 3 years from his 18th birthday in which to commence proceedings if these have not already been brought. So, a child who is injured at the age of two may have another 19 years in which to bring a claim.

in Scotland
Actions of damages for personal injury must generally be brought within 3 years. In exceptional cases, the court allows actions to be brought later, but you should not rely on this. Your right to bring an action for other kinds of damage (such as damage to property) lapses after 5 years from the date of damage.

The 3-year period starts on the latest of

○ the date when you were injured
○ the date when the continuing act or omission which caused your injuries ceased
○ the date when you were, or ought to have been, aware of both the seriousness of your injuries and the fact that they were caused by the defender's acts or omissions.

It ends when you commence a court action, or, more precisely, when you serve on the defender the summons or initial writ setting out your claims.

Any time during which the pursuer is under the age of 18 or of unsound mind does not count towards the 3-year period.

Girls under 12 or boys under 14 cannot sue for themselves. Normally their parents sue on their behalf. Older children who are under 18 can themselves sue but have to have the consent of their parents.

Where a child has no parent, or the parent refuses to act or has an adverse interest, the court appoints someone else (called a *curator ad litem*) to act on behalf of the child or to consent to the child's proceedings.

professional advice

You may not be sure whether the circumstances of your accident justify making a claim for compensation from the person who caused it. If you are in any doubt at all, you should seek professional advice as soon as possible. Normally the appropriate person to consult would be a solicitor.

In cases where an accident has involved injury to anyone under the age of 18, you must consult a lawyer. No one under the age of 18 can pursue a claim in person but has to sue through someone who is called the 'next friend'. This is usually a parent or guardian who has to apply to the court to be appointed 'next friend' in order to bring the proceedings on behalf of the child.

Even if you are quite sure that you have a case, you should get a solicitor's help. People who think they can do it themselves may get into deep water and then find that they have to ask for professional advice, only to be told that because of some step that they have taken, they have seriously prejudiced their claim.

The local citizens advice bureau or a legal advice centre may be able to give you some preliminary advice and can tell you about various schemes which enable you to get the advice of a solicitor at either minimal or, in some cases, no cost to yourself. Some citizens advice bureaux (CABx) provide a legal advice 'surgery' staffed by qualified lawyers on one or more days a week.

If you are a member of a trade union, you may well be able to get advice through your union representative, not only on an accident sustained at work but on other liability claims as well.

The Law Society is setting up an Accident Legal Advice Service (ALAS!) which offers victims of an accident an initial free interview with a solicitor for advice on whether there is a good case for claiming compensation. Leaflets about ALAS! are available at citizens advice bureaux, local libraries and other information points. If you send the coupon attached to the leaflet to the local Law Society (address on leaflet) or take it to a solicitor in the area who participates in the scheme, you will be given an appointment for a free interview.

An alternative Law Society scheme is the 'fixed-fee' interview. The local citizens advice bureau will tell you which of the solicitors in the town offer this service. Basically, the solicitor offers you 30 minutes of his time for a fixed fee of £5 inclusive of VAT. This will enable the solicitor to ascertain whether you have a claim and should pursue your case, and to give you guidelines as to what action you should take. The time allowed will not enable the solicitor to embark on the conduct of your case himself. If you overshoot the allotted half-hour, you then pay at his normal rate.

choosing a solicitor

It is important to choose the right solicitor. There is no point in going to a divorce or conveyancing specialist for a damages claim. Personal injury is a complicated area of law, if not in terms of legal theory, certainly in terms of legal practice. It is a minefield of tactical manoeuvring with many pitfalls for the inexperienced.

A good way of finding a solicitor is through recommendation from a friend or relative who has actually used that solicitor for a similar type of case and has been satisfied.

If you know nobody who can recommend a solicitor, you can find names of some solicitors in the area by going through a classified telephone directory such as the Yellow Pages or Thomsons and by looking at solicitors' advertisements.

The Law Society's regional directories of solicitors are available in CABx, public libraries and court offices throughout the country. Each regional directory lists solicitors practising in the particular area who have given information about their availability, whether they are willing to undertake legal aid cases and/or give 'fixed-fee' interviews or participate in the accident legal advice service, and indicating the category of work they are prepared to undertake (look for the category 'accident claims' or 'litigation – accidents'). Since virtually every firm in the country will handle accident claims to some degree, the guidance from this list may be of limited value: the list merely indicates the willingness of the solicitor to do that sort of work, not his experience.

When making your appointment with the firm of solicitors you have chosen, explain briefly the nature of your problem and ask that you be dealt with by somebody who specialises in this type of work. It is easy for what appears to be a simple case to become complicated, and you may need someone who can deal with the more sophisticated or complex aspects of personal injury work. The 'other side' is likely to be, effectively, insurers and their claims assessors and their solicitors, who are always specialists, and who can run rings round inexperienced solicitors. Do not be afraid to challenge the solicitor as to his experience. Ask "how many personal injury cases do you do a year?" and "when was the last?". Some solicitors who profess to be experienced may rely on obtaining a barrister's advice, at your expense.

legal advice scheme

If your income and savings are below certain limits, you may find that you are eligible for the statutory legal advice and assistance scheme. The scheme is known as the 'green form' scheme because of the colour of the application form (pink in Scotland). If you are in receipt of supplementary benefit (SB) or family income supplement (FIS) you are automatically eligible.

The green form scheme is intended to provide initial advice and assistance for people of small or moderate means; in particular, advice on whether they have a claim worth pursuing.

Unless you are on SB or FIS, the solicitor will ask about your and your spouse's financial means (gross weekly income, any savings or capital) and your outgoings and dependants. From this information, he can let you know whether you are eligible. If so, he will complete the application form, which you will have to sign, confirming that the information given is correct and that you accept the terms of the scheme.

If your disposable income is within a given range, you will have to pay to the solicitor straight away a contribution towards the scheme. This is a single payment, from £5 upwards, scaled according to your income. (The eligibility limits and the scale for contributions are regularly reviewed and updated.)

The scheme enables the solicitor to give you up to £50-worth of advice. He is paid by the Law Society at a fixed hourly rate which currently allows him to give you about $1\frac{3}{4}$ hours of his time. This should enable the solicitor to advise whether you have a claim and how you should pursue it, and perhaps to write a few letters on your behalf. In anything but the most straightforward circumstances, it is not enough for him to see the claim through for you. The solicitor cannot, under the scheme, make any appearance in court to represent you.

legal aid scheme
You may also be financially eligible for the legal aid scheme. Under the scheme, which is funded by the state and administered by the Law Society (in Scotland, by the Scottish Legal Aid Board), an eligible applicant gets the services of a solicitor (and barrister, where appropriate) free or on payment of an assessed contribution towards the cost.

In order to obtain legal aid for a claim, it will be necessary for you to show that you have a *prima facie* case. It is unlikely to be granted for a claim for damages of less than £500.

The legal aid application has to be made through your solicitor; it goes to the legal aid area office to assess the legal merits of your case and the DHSS to see if your financial means make you eligible. The application may take some while to be processed, perhaps several months.

The solicitor should discuss the question of legal aid at your first interview. Many people qualify, although they may have to pay a contribution towards their legal costs under the scheme.

If eligible, you will be offered a legal aid certificate, on condition that you pay any contribution required on the basis of your disposable income and disposable capital. From then on, your legal costs are covered by the scheme. Any costs that your solicitor incurs prior to the issue of the legal aid certificate will be your responsibility. It may be difficult for the solicitor to apply for legal aid for you until he has discovered more about your case, and he will ask you to pay for the work (except for work covered by the 'green form' advice scheme).

The certificate may be limited to taking the case up to a certain stage in the proceedings. If you wish to continue, the solicitor must show again that the case has a good chance of success (this may mean obtaining a barrister's opinion).

All offers to settle out of court must be notified to the legal aid area office. The office may withdraw legal aid if they think a reasonable offer has been refused.

If you succeed in being paid damages as a result of the litigation for which you are legally aided, this sum will be subject to the 'statutory legal aid charge' to meet the costs of the case paid by the legal aid fund. The solicitor should explain to you at the outset how the statutory charge will affect what you may get. Your solicitor will have to retain all the money received in damages and pay out of this to the Law Society what the case has cost the legal aid scheme and you then get the balance. In a successful personal injury claim, however, this may not be a problem because the bulk of the successful party's costs will normally be payable by the other side.

An advantage of legal aid is that if you lose your case, you have no further liability for costs beyond any contribution you have been required to make. Furthermore, in most cases you will not have to pay the other party's costs, or the court will limit the amount you have to pay and order that it be paid by instalments.

Leaflets about the legal aid and advice schemes are available at solicitors' offices and citizens advice bureaux, and from the legal aid head office, Newspaper House, 8–16 Great New Street, London EC4 3BN.

insurance for legal expenses

If you have an insurance policy covering legal expenses, check without delay whether the circumstances of your case enable you to claim on this, and what procedure is laid down for claiming. Such insurance indemnifies you for the legal costs of a case (with specified exceptions), whether as plaintiff or defendant.

The insurance is either a separate policy for legal expenses or an add-on extension to another policy, such as household, or motor for claiming 'uninsured losses' from another person. A 'family' policy will cover members of the family living permanently with the policyholder (there may be an age limit of 21 for 'children'), so you may be able to benefit from a parent's or a spouse's prescience.

Some have a waiting period of 3 months from the date of

taking out a policy before you can claim: an accident giving rise to a claim within that period would not be covered.

The policies have different exclusions and conditions but a claim for damages for personal injury or damaged property after an accident should come within the criteria of all policies.

Most of the firms providing this cover offer a 24-hour telephone advisory service free to policyholders, so you can get some preliminary guidance on the steps to take.

You must tell your insurers as soon as you think you will be needing to claim; check whether there is a time limit in your policy (for instance, 180 days) for notifying an impending claim. None will accept a case that, in the judgment of the insurers, does not have a reasonable chance of succeeding.

The policy is strictly for legal expenses, so you cannot make use of it unless you are prepared to have a solicitor to pursue your claim. You will have to get the insurers' approval of the solicitor you want to go to. Some insurers will instruct a solicitor on your behalf.

Solicitors' fees and expenses are met irrespective of whether the case goes to court or is settled by negotiation (which is likely to be cheaper for the insurers). If you win your case and costs are ordered to be paid by the other side, these have to be paid over to the insurers.

There is a ceiling on the amount that will be met per claim (£25,000 with most policies, or less for a lower premium) and some have a maximum for claims within the year.

Once you are using the insurance, the insurers will have to be informed before any major expenditure is undertaken (for instance, getting a barrister in or consulting an expensive expert) and of any offer of settlement. If you turn down what they think is a good offer, they may not cover your further legal expenses in trying to get more.

If a dispute arises between you and the insurers about the handling of the claim or, in particular, accepting a negotiated settlement, you can request that the matter be referred to arbitration. If the arbitrator decides against you, you will be responsible for paying the costs of the arbitration.

using a solicitor

Once you have decided on a solicitor, it is better not to take any further action such as writing to the opposition until you have seen the solicitor. A badly worded letter by a claimant can cause a cock-up and then the solicitor has to try and salvage a case which should have been a good one.

You should always make an appointment before going to see your solicitor. Do not simply drop in and expect him to forget all about his other clients and see you. Unnecessary visits to a solicitor will increase the costs you have to pay and decrease the likelihood of their being recovered from the other side.

Solicitors charge by the hour, and they are not cheap. Do not, therefore, waste money by wasting time. You should try to ensure that when you go to see your solicitor on each occasion you are prepared for the appointment. Do not take offence if the solicitor seeks to keep the interview short – he is probably looking after your interests better than one who is happy to sit back and talk generalities.

information needed when going to see a solicitor

On your first visit, you should give your solicitor a brief outline of the case. Tell him everything that has happened as a result of the accident, even if you are not sure whether it is relevant, and let him judge what is and is not important. He will ask you what else he needs to know.

Do not fail to take with you to the solicitor any correspondence that you may have had with other parties and any supporting documents that might be relevant.

Be prepared to tell him

○ your full names, date of birth, normal occupation
○ address and telephone number
○ date, time and place of accident (if appropriate, details of cars involved, make and registration numbers, road conditions)

- injuries suffered by you
- details of anybody else injured
- details and value of any damaged property
- name and address of person who caused accident, and details of his insurance (if known)
- if relevant, name and address of own insurers and policy number
- if accident at work, details of subsequent action taken by employers (such as putting protection round machinery)
- witnesses' names and addresses and what they saw (if known)
- notes taken by you immediately after accident
- any photographs, sketch plans
- action taken since accident, including copies of any correspondence
- name and number of any police officer involved, and name of police station, if known
- details of expenses incurred as result of accident
- details of salary etc lost as result of accident (payslips)
- hospital attended, with name of doctor (if known), whether X-rays taken
- name and address of your general practitioner
- for legal aid purposes, your capital, income and outgoings, spouse's earnings and capital; details of any previous application for legal aid
- if relevant, supplementary benefit reference number and address of social security office.

But do not delay going to see a solicitor just because you do not have all the information.

delays

There will almost certainly be a number of delays in your case; probably your solicitor will not be able to do anything about some of these. Delay of many weeks from the date of your application for legal aid to the granting of the legal aid certificate is only one of them.

There are also delays in waiting for replies to come back from insurance companies (who themselves may experience difficulties and delays in obtaining information from their insured and others), tracing witnesses and then interviewing them, waiting for you to see a medical consultant who may have a 3-month waiting list.

Do not blame the solicitor for delays that are outside his control but ask him for the precise reasons for any delay. At all times, make sure that your solicitor keeps you fully informed. It may be useful to keep a log yourself of what happens and when.

If you have any queries at any time, do not hesitate to raise them with the solicitor. Part of the problem which solicitors face is that clients frequently do not raise queries which are worrying them. Bear in mind that one of the reasons why your solicitor may appear to be acting slowly is that he is not getting proper instructions from you. Do not ignore his requests for information. You must help by not wasting time and by dealing with points that he requests be dealt with as promptly as possible.

You should not assume that cautious advice from your solicitor indicates lack of interest. But if you become disillusioned with your solicitor because he does not keep you informed or has to be pushed at each stage, you should consider finding another solicitor to take on the case for you. Should you be in receipt of legal aid, however, you will need the authority of the local legal aid committee before the case can be transferred to another solicitor.

what you can claim for

A claim arising out of an accident is for damages: those losses which arise solely and directly as a result of the accident and are reasonably foreseeable. The aim is to place you in the same position as far as possible as you would have been in had the accident not occurred.

There are two categories of damages for which you can claim: 'special' and 'general' damages. **In Scotland**, special damages are called damages for patrimonial loss and the equivalent of general damages is solatium; both are often loosely referred to as damages.

special damages

Special damages are payable to compensate you for a direct financial loss that you have sustained, for which a precise figure is available.

This would include net loss of earnings, cost of repairs to car, value of damaged clothing, taxi fares, any other expenses that can be specifically itemised. Nobody is going to compensate you unless you can show that you have actually incurred those expenses, so you should keep a note of the amounts spent and keep receipts. If you have receipts to produce, it is likely that those sums at least will not be in dispute.

All reasonable costs of treatment necessary as a result of the accident will normally be allowed, whether private or under the NHS. This includes the cost of drugs or appliances and the cost of getting to and from treatment, as well as any medical fees.

private medical treatment
The cost of private medical treatment is recoverable as special damages, provided the treatment was necessary and the cost

not unreasonable or excessive. The fact that the treatment would have been available under the NHS does not debar such a claim.

The cost of private physiotherapy can be claimed for. Physiotherapy may be more readily obtained outside the NHS, and more conveniently arranged – for example, to fit in with working hours. The fees of practitioners such as osteopath or chiropractor can also be claimed as special damages.

Members of private medical schemes, such as BUPA or PPP, who claim medical expenses from the scheme following an accident and gain recovery of those medical expenses from a negligent third party, are required under a condition imposed by the schemes to refund to the scheme the appropriate amount from the damages awarded.

other losses

It may be that, as a result of the accident, you are unable to carry out those activities in the household which you have been accustomed to doing, and that you have to pay someone else to do so. You will have to have medical evidence to support the view that you are unable to carry out those chores – and receipts from the person you paid to do them.

Essentially, a claim for damages is for your own loss arising as a result of the accident. However, there are some circumstances where there may be a claim on behalf of another person's loss arising out of your injury: for example, if you have an elderly relative who is wholly dependent on you for all sorts of services, you may be able to claim for the cost of employing somebody else to provide those services. It would normally be necessary to show some legal or strong moral obligation to carry out such services – close family relationship would probably be enough. This is never a clear-cut situation and you may have difficulty in recovering all of the expenses incurred.

If a husband (or wife) loses earnings because of having to

take unpaid time off work to look after the injured spouse, this financial loss counts for special damages.

If an accident arises immediately before a holiday so that you cannot go on it, you may be able to claim for your lost deposit or the cost of an unusable air ticket or for money lost as the result of your being unable to cancel the holiday within the time required by the tour operator. However, if you have already been paid for lost deposit or air tickets or hotel accommodation under a holiday travel policy, you must pay back to the holiday travel insurers any amounts in this respect that you recover from the person at fault. The same applies to any amounts you may recover under any other policy of indemnity – for example, for car repairs under your own comprehensive motor policy. The reason for this is that, in law, you are not entitled to recover for the same loss twice; if you did not pay the amounts back this would amount to fraud.

general damages

Part of your claim will be for 'general damages', to compensate you in financial terms for the pain and suffering which have been caused.

Unlike special damages where you claim a precise amount for each item, for general damages you do not specify exact figures but list the factors for which you seek compensation: the pain or suffering, the physical effect, including any cosmetic effect, that you have had to endure and may still have to endure, and the foreseeable risk of later ill effects.

The claim includes the loss of amenity – that is, that since the accident you have not been able, and may not ever again be able, to perform all the tasks and activities that you normally did. The loss of amenity claimed can include restriction on pursuing a hobby.

It is extremely difficult to compensate such matters in financial terms, and you must seek proper legal advice on the matter.

A claim for general damages will have to be supported by medical evidence showing that you have sustained those injuries and in what way and for how long the injuries are likely to affect you.

future loss

General damages also include compensation for any future loss of earnings or other future financial losses (such as reduced pension where prolonged absence from work will affect contributions and result in a lower pension). Damages for 'loss of earning capacity' or 'disadvantage on the open labour market' can be claimed, where appropriate. This means the risk that if your present employment is lost because of injury sustained in the accident, you will have difficulty in obtaining other employment of a similar nature at similar wages.

For assessing loss of future earning capacity, the court will seek to establish the likely level of future annual earnings (ignoring the effect of inflation) and will then normally apply what is called a 'multiplier' to that figure, based on age and reasonable life or earning expectancy. The court will take into account that you will be getting your money earlier than had you not had the accident, and will give a discount for 'accelerated payment' so that the multiplier will be significantly less than the actual future period of employment.

General damages also include future expenses which are likely to arise or continue, such as future medical expenses and replacement of special equipment. The amount awarded depends on the time over which these are expected to continue.

In Scotland, a specific sum has to be claimed for solatium although you do not have to quantify it by reference to bills paid, earnings lost etc. The judge may award you less than the sum you claim but is not permitted to award you more.

interest

You are entitled to ask for interest on any damages which are awarded to you for the time it has taken for your claim to reach court or to settle. Strictly, interest is only available where a case goes to trial but it is usually taken into account in other cases.

Entitlement to interest begins to run from the date of issue of legal proceedings in the case of general damages, and from the accident in the case of special damages. In some cases, however, an insurance company may agree that provided you do not issue proceedings, they will accept that any interest on general damages should run from the date of that agreement, as if proceedings had been started then.

FIRST STEPS

You should act promptly, but be prepared to wait a long time after the accident before you get any compensation. Do not expect it to be settled in a few months; it is better to face the fact right at the beginning that it could take a year – or even two or more.

This is partly due to the procedural aspects which have to be resolved, partly to solicitors' delays, partly to insurers needing to establish their insured's liability through investigation; witnesses have to be traced and interviewed; professional and expert reports awaited; police reports, where relevant, released. And if the case proceeds to court, there is the court's waiting list.

who to claim on

There is little point in starting a claim if the person who is responsible is unlikely to be able to pay up either from his own resources or through an insurance policy. Apart from motor insurance which is compulsory for causing personal injury, some other insurance policies provide personal liability cover, which the policyholder may not be aware of – for example, under a householder's contents policy. But your legal right is to sue the person who caused you the injury or loss and not his or her insurers.

In many accident claims, liability is clear cut, but you should be prepared to assume that liability will be disputed. Insurers are not likely to pay out any money before they have ascertained the precise liability of their insured.

If you believe you have a good case (and you must be realistic about this), do not be deterred. Most insurers are also realistic, and persistence will usually result in a settlement, often without the need for court action. Even if legal proceedings have to be started, it does not follow that the case will go to trial.

Once you have given your solicitor the facts about the accident, he can write to the person whom you hold responsible for the accident saying that you intend to proceed with a claim for damages for your loss and injuries and suggesting that he ought to pass the letter to his insurers.

Insurers cannot enter the arena unless the policyholder asks them to handle the claim. You cannot make a claim direct to someone else's insurers.

Most insurance policies have a clause giving the insurers the right to take over a claim entirely. The insurers will then stand in the shoes of the defendant. The claim itself is made against the defendant but he will be there in name only: the party who will conduct the case, instruct solicitors and so forth, will be the insurers and all correspondence will be with them or their solicitors.

Knowing that a claim will be dealt with by insurers and their solicitors should help to overcome the understandable reluctance or embarrassment when the person you should be claiming on is a close friend or colleague or member of the family. You may not need to have any direct contact with him or her during the proceedings, and any payment that you get will not be coming from his or her pocket.

preparing evidence

The essential elements involved in supporting a claim are to show that you have suffered damage as a result of the negligence of the other party.

You must seek evidence in support of your claim from the very first, bearing in mind that much evidence may disappear with the passage of time.

evidence of what happened

Immediately after an accident you are unlikely to be thinking clearly: any injury (except the most minor) will produce shock and disorientation, as well as the pain of the injury itself.

Beware of making any statement to any other party which could be interpreted as an admission of your own liability. It is far better to say nothing than to incriminate yourself. If you can get the other person to sign a statement at the scene of the accident, saying that everything was his fault, this may be helpful. If liability is admitted by one party then, this may enable the matter to proceed in a fairly straightforward manner – although the court may well look cautiously at an admission of liability made 'in the agony of the moment'.

If you are too shocked or upset to make notes there and then of what happened, you should record your version of what happened by writing out a statement as soon as possible after the incident, when you are calmer. Do so while the events are still fresh in your mind. The passage of time would seriously affect your evidence, so the sooner that you are able to make your own statement the better, and it will be more accurate. Moreover, a document may only be referred to when giving evidence in court if it was prepared at the time of, or very shortly after, the incident and can be regarded as contemporaneous. That is why you should always make a note of the precise date and time at which you write these notes.

Do not give your statement to the other person. It may

unwittingly contain something not to your advantage, and may harm your case if the other side gets hold of it.

Your solicitor will almost certainly want to take a full statement from you at an early stage.

The following is the sort of evidence that you should try to have in order to support your claim.

statements of witnesses

At the time of the accident you (or, if you are not in a fit state to do so, someone with you) should take down the names and addresses of all witnesses of the accident. Your solicitor can then take statements from the witnesses of their version of events as soon as possible. The greater the number of witnesses who support your version, the more likely you are to succeed.

If anyone else has been injured or had property damaged from the same incident, keep in touch with them. You can be useful as each other's witness.

photographs

Photographs of the place in which the accident occurred will be an advantage. Taken at the time, they may be invaluable. But there are few cases where you are likely to have your camera available to you at the precise moment that the accident occurred. In most cases, it would be advisable to return to the accident spot as soon as possible thereafter in order to take photographs. Then you, or a friend who is a better photographer, can take a series of shots from different angles at your leisure.

Take a ruler or other measure as part of the photograph so that the precise extent of the defect can be seen from the photo. Keep the ruler or other measure in case there is at a later stage a dispute over the accuracy of the measurement.

It is helpful to prepare a sketch plan of the scene of the accident with relevant measurements and indicate on the plan the position from which each photograph was taken and the direction in which it was taken.

You can send a copy of your photographs to the opposition and invite them to agree them. If they do not, either they can take their own set of photographs or you and they can go back to the scene and take photographs together.

In the case of defective premises where the defect is apparent, a comprehensive set of photographs can be of assistance in establishing your claim. If your claim is for an injury as a result of falling because of a hole in the highway, for example, a photograph will be useful.

Act quickly. You may find that the defect gets rapidly repaired. A possible negligence claim is a great incentive to a sudden decision that repairs should be done. A photograph of a neatly repaired roof is not a great deal of help as evidence that there were loose tiles two days earlier, that fell when you happened to be underneath.

evidence of injuries

Your solicitor will discuss with you what medical evidence will be required.

If you have attended a hospital (perhaps in the first instance) in the casualty department), a report from the doctor who saw you may be helpful. This will basically be a résumé of his notes. You can write to the hospital administrator, quoting your hospital number and the dates of your attendance, and request such a report. This is usually provided fairly quickly; the charge will be in the region of £40 to £60. This report will briefly set out the injuries that you had when you attended the hospital and the treatment that you received and any recommendations made to you. This is important as it shows the way in which your injuries appeared at the time of, or shortly after, the incident.

GP's report

You may want a report from your general practitioner. Normally this will be a short report prepared from his notes made when seeing you. When you first go to see your GP about your injury, tell him or her that it was due to an accident and what happened. Doctors are much more likely to write down all their findings if they think a legal case is likely to follow and that they may be asked to provide a report. Otherwise, symptoms or findings may be summarised very briefly by the doctor in his or her notes and they may be of less use than they otherwise might have been.

His report should set out the injuries that you had at the time you went to him, the reasons for your consulting him, the treatment that you received and any recommendations that he has made. It will not normally indicate how the injuries may resolve. The doctor can charge a fee for such a report. If a forecast of the result of the injuries is sought or any further opinion required of him, the fee will normally be higher.

People sometimes find old symptoms are aggravated through an accident even if there may be little objective clinical evidence to support their claim. Ensure that the solicitor has all the medical facts, including your past medical history. Even if it appears a previous injury may be relevant and harm your case, it is better that it is brought out by 'your' expert and considered sympathetically at an early stage. The new injury may exacerbate previous problems or an earlier injury and may contribute to greater risk of later ill effects. An example is whiplash injury to the neck: neck injuries are common and can easily be aggravated by, for example, collision in a motor vehicle.

specialists' reports
You will almost inevitably need to obtain expert reports, prepared by a consultant in the particular sphere. It is often advisable to get a medical report from a doctor or consultant who is independent and not involved in your treatment and who is accustomed to providing medical reports for personal injury claims.

A medical report by the GP which is too general and overoptimistic about the length of time the injury would take to heal might be used by the other side's insurers to set lower compensation. An advantage of getting a report from a doctor not immediately treating you is that doctors must assume that a cure is possible for their patients; they are not willing nor, without affecting the doctor-patient relationship, psychologically able to admit that there may not be a cure or complete recovery.

Your solicitor should be able to find the appropriate consultant or doctor who is known regularly to provide medico/legal reports: for example, where the injury is to the teeth or the jaw, the opinion of an orthodontist will be required.

Your solicitor should arrange for you to see the appropriately qualified specialist. You may have to make a special visit to the hospital to see the consultant so that he can assess your injuries, the likelihood of any permanent disability or the possibility of future treatment. You will be asked by your solicitor to sign a statement giving your permission for the consultant to release medical information to the solicitor.

You must expect to pay handsomely for the specialist's services. If you are successful in your claim, this expenditure should be refunded by your opponent as part of your costs. (If you have a legal aid certificate, this will cover the cost of specialist reports.)

The specialist's report will not only set out injuries received, but will also attempt to give some form of prediction as to the outcome of those injuries, the treatment required, whether they are likely to resolve completely and, if not, what amenities are likely to have been lost. The value of such a report cannot be underestimated: your solicitor cannot pursue a claim if he does not have the medical evidence available to him.

Medical reports are normally 'disclosed' (that is, shown) to the other side at some point in the proceedings. You are entitled to withhold a medical report or that part of it which does not say what you particularly want it to say. But you are unlikely to establish any basis for negotiation or achieve any settlement without disclosing a full medical report. The other side may have suspicions about the strength of your claim if you are not open with them.

report for the other side
Your opponent is entitled to ask that you be examined by his own expert to check the nature of your injuries. It would be pointless to refuse to submit to such an examination, but you should agree only on the understanding that the report will be disclosed. You should be honest with the doctor even though he is instructed by your opponent. You may have to have a number of examinations and reports in the course of proceedings.

The other side will have to pay the expenses of such examinations. But if you lose the case, they will be able to recover all such costs from you, or from the institution funding your case (such as your trade union).

medical photographs
If you have received injuries with any sort of visible effect, photographs are useful. They should be taken as soon as possible after the injury has been received to show any swelling or bruising which was caused.

If the injuries are likely to take some time to heal, a series of photographs should, if at all feasible, be taken to plot how the injuries develop. You should make a careful note of the dates on which the photographs are taken.

Where scars, bruises and so forth are concerned, it is very important that photographs show them in detail, and in their best – or worst – light. A professional photographer will know the way in which this can best be done. The majority of hospitals have medical photography departments – photographs of injuries are regularly taken and used as part of the medical records. If requested by a solicitor, such medical photographs can be taken or made available. The hospital will charge for this service.

Photographs taken before the injuries were received can be a help in determining the extent of those injuries. If you have some photographs of yourself, taken as recently as possible before the accident, show them to the photographer who is taking the new photographs. He can then try to take at least one or two shots which match up with the old photographs, from the same angle and showing the same pose, so that the precise difference can be seen.

your claim for damages

Generally speaking, an entirely different approach will be taken to the calculation of damages in a case leading to permanent disability as a result of the accident (where there will be ongoing expenses or additional needs for the remainder of the person's life), and a case when the person concerned will recover fully within a period of weeks or months (where the injury involves temporary inconvenience and an end can be seen to any expenses and damages arising out of it).

evidence for special damages

The booklet *Disability and compensation claims* (published by Sweet and Maxwell, 1986 edition £5.95) deals with general points in calculating expenses, and has sections on spinal injury, partial and total loss of sight, loss of a limb, head injury, giving costs of special equipment, adaptations and expenses of additional care and attendance required.

You should accumulate the evidence of the exact amounts you have spent, such as receipts for car hire, for medical treatment, special equipment. You may have to get in the habit of asking for receipts where these are not normally given – from the hairdresser, taxi driver, dry cleaner, for example. If valuable property has been damaged beyond replacement or repair, an expert's valuation may be required. Special damages can cover matters such as home nursing care, special equipment (wheelchair, standing device, bathing aid), housing alterations and other such items.

Only reasonable expenses will be allowed. A claimant is under a duty to 'mitigate his loss' – that is, take steps to keep it as low as possible.

loss of earnings

In most cases, an employee can support a claim for loss of pay by producing payslips over a period of, say, twelve months before the accident or until the employer stopped paying full wages. This can also be evidence in support of a claim for lost bonuses and overtime. The claim has to be for loss of take-home pay, after tax and other deductions such as pension contributions, not gross pay. Account is also taken of social security benefits received during the period of your claim.

In the case of a self-employed person, loss of earnings can be difficult to quantify. A claim will have to be based on loss of profit due to the effect of the accident on your working ability. If you are self-employed or work freelance, you should get from your accountant properly prepared accounts to support your claim for loss of profit or earnings over the time that you are unable to work. In many businesses, seasonal and various other fluctuations affect the takings or profit; this may become a matter for negotiation.

evidence for general damages

General damages can be more difficult to substantiate by virtue of their vague nature.

An element taken into account when deciding on the award for general damages is the foreseeable risk of further or later complications arising from the injury. Even if recovery from the present injury is virtually complete, the medical report(s) should forecast any deterioration or associated condition (for example, epilepsy or arthritis) that it can reasonably be assumed will develop as a direct result.

Evidence relevant for claiming general damages may include

statements from friends and/or from employers as to loss of amenity or how your personality has changed. You yourself should record what pain and discomfort you experienced during the period of recovery. Each case will require its own individual supporting evidence.

Some injuries take a long time to heal. Until it can be known precisely what injury has been suffered and its prognosis and the disability that will be involved in the future, no final assessment of compensation can be made. Because claims are settled on a 'once and for all basis', it is important to obtain a detailed medical report and prognosis before final settlement terms are discussed.

Except in very rare circumstances, once a case is settled, it cannot be re-opened. Once you have received compensation, be it through the court or through negotiated settlement, you cannot normally receive compensation again for the same injury even if further complications arise later.

TAKING YOUR CASE FURTHER

You must be prepared for the fact that what you and your solicitor think is a good case and a fair claim and what your opponent thinks is a good case and a fair settlement are likely to be two very different things. It may therefore be that your case will have to proceed to court.

Your solicitor may decide to instruct a barrister (referred to as 'counsel', advocate in Scotland) to advise on your case and possibly prepare some of the documents. Even a solicitor specialising in accident and personal injury claims may get counsel's advice on evidence when proceedings are under way and it looks as though the case is going to court. Some solicitors will, as a matter of routine, get counsel's opinion on general damages.

The mere fact that proceedings have been started does not mean that the case will eventually be heard in court. The majority of cases relating to accidents and personal injury are settled at some stage without coming to a hearing.

Settlements are reached by bargaining which often depends on the relative strengths of the parties. Insurers may start by making the minimum offer they think the claimant will accept. The claimant must weigh the advantages of a smaller but certain sum now, compared with an uncertain larger amount at some unspecified date in the future.

Where a final settlement is achieved on behalf of a child without a final court hearing, the court has to be asked to give its approval to any agreement reached between the parties.

Where there are protracted delaying tactics, there is much to be said for starting court proceedings (in Scotland, raising an action). Once the case is subject to the jurisdiction of the court, both parties are tied down by various time limits which may speed up any negotiations for settlement and bring an element of realism and speed into a case.

court procedure

The first step is to issue a summons in the county court or a writ in the High Court (sheriff court or Court of Session in Scotland). With it goes a document called the 'statement of claim' in the High Court and the 'particulars of claim' in the county court; they are similar, and are referred to as pleadings.

The document is prepared by your solicitor but you should make sure to see it. It should set out basically what the claim is about, naming both parties (plaintiff and defendant), stating the date on which the accident occurred, the circumstances in which the accident occurred and why it is alleged that the other party is responsible in negligence for the accident. It will then go on to state what damages have been sustained by the plaintiff and what he is claiming.

Once the pleadings have been issued and served on the other party (the defendant), he has to acknowledge them (in the High Court) within a stipulated number of days and has an opportunity to reply ('serve a defence') within a further set time stating what, if any, of the statement of claim is denied or admitted; he can allege contributory negligence on the plaintiff's part. The plaintiff can dispute the defendant's defence.

The pleadings, chiefly the particulars or statement of claim and the defence, do not have to state the evidence. Evidence of witnesses has to be given orally at the hearing except in the case of expert witnesses. Experts' reports will probably be exchanged at some time during the case in order to be agreed before the case comes to hearing, so that you do not need to call those experts in person to give evidence in court and thus avoid the expenses of this. Unless experts' reports have been exchanged between the parties before the hearing, these reports cannot be produced as evidence at the hearing and the expert witnesses have to attend court.

'discovery'

Documentary evidence and details of all relevant documents are made known ('disclosed') by a procedure known as 'discovery'. The idea is to save time in court and to ensure that neither party is taken by surprise and that before the matter comes to court, each party will be aware in broad terms what claims are being made by the other, and has a proper opportunity to prepare the case.

Discovery basically requires each party to serve on the other a list of all relevant documents which are or have been in that party's possession or power. The other party is then entitled to ask for discovery and inspect the documents. Contemporaneous notes, statements, police reports, accident reports, accident investigation reports, evidence of previous similar accidents can be very relevant. In the case of road accidents, the plaintiff (and the defendant if he makes a counterclaim) must give discovery of documents relating to his damages claim.

It is quite common for discovery to be dealt with informally by the plaintiff sending to the defendant copies of any bills, invoices, estimates etc supporting the various sums claimed.

In Scotland, too, there is 'discovery': before the pleadings are finalised, each party must, if required, lodge in court all documents in their possession supporting their case.

payment into court

At some stage in the case, the defendant may make a payment of money 'into court', to be held by the court pending the outcome of the case. This is in effect a formal offer of compensation. The plaintiff is notified and has 21 days (High Court) or 14 days (in the county court) in which to accept this payment. If he does, that ends the case: he takes the money and tells the court that he withdraws the claim, and gets payment of his costs up to that time.

If he does not accept, the money remains with the court and the case proceeds. The judge will not know if there has been a payment into court until after he has made his decision. If, at the final hearing, the plaintiff is awarded a sum of money which is equal to or less than the payment into court, he will have to pay not only his own costs but also the other side's costs from the date of the payment into court. These are likely substantially to exceed the earlier costs as they normally include the costs of finally preparing the case, including counsel's fees and the charge for solicitors' attendance and expert witnesses. The defendant may be ordered to pay the plaintiff's costs up to that date.

The practice is a departure from the usual rule that the successful party is entitled to have his costs paid by the other party. The plaintiff is penalised for having wasted everybody's time by coming to court when he could have had the same amount of money (or more) far earlier.

In Scotland, instead of paying money into court, the defender merely offers to pay a certain sum in order to settle the case. This is called a tender and has the same effect on liability for subsequent expenses as a payment into court has in England and Wales.

at the trial

Should your case proceed to a court hearing, the judge will have read the pleadings (that is, the court papers which set out the case for each party) and any agreed reports from experts.

The plaintiff's lawyer 'opens' the case by giving a description of his client's case. The detailed specific facts will have to come from witnesses who are called to give oral evidence in court.

Briefly, a witness is first of all questioned by the lawyer acting for the party on whose behalf he is giving evidence. This questioning – called examination in chief – is designed to bring out the details of the accident, putting particular stress on those parts of the evidence which help the party calling the witness. The witness is then cross-examined by the opponent's lawyer, who will seek to persuade the witness that he is mistaken or forgetful, or did not have a clear view of the accident, or in some other way to minimise those parts of his evidence which are harmful to the other party's case. He may then be re-examined by his own side's lawyer to try to put right any damage caused by cross-examination.

The plaintiff and his witness(es) give evidence first, each being examined, cross-examined and re-examined. If there are agreed expert or medical reports, these are read to the court. If the reports are not agreed, the experts have to give evidence in person, in the usual way.

The defendant, his witnesses and expert witnesses then give evidence. After that, the lawyer for the defendant closes the case for the defence by putting arguments and submissions before the judge; he is followed by the lawyer for the plaintiff doing likewise.

The defendant does not have to show that he was not at fault: it is up to the plaintiff to prove his case. This burden of proof should not be underestimated. You may know that you are telling the truth but the judge's decision can be made only on the evidence available to him, both with regard to liability and on the quantum (amount) of your claim.

When giving his decision, the judge will deal with all the relevant points and may indicate that he prefers the evidence of one witness over that of another. The judge has to decide on the evidence he has heard whether the plaintiff's case is more likely than the defendant's. The standard which the judge has to apply is one of a balance of probabilities, not one of certainty as in a criminal case, and he can take into account any contributory negligence on the part of the plaintiff.

You must face the possibility that the judge may not find in your favour and, as well as not being awarded any compensation, you may well end up being ordered to pay the other side's legal costs.

costs

If you are successful at the end of the trial, your solicitor should ask for an order that the unsuccessful party should pay costs.

In most cases you will, under the present rules as to costs, be able to recover a substantial part of the costs and disbursements your solicitor charges you.

In addition to your solicitor's charges, you can include your expenses of supporting your claim: fees for medical reports, for experts' evidence, photographs, telephone calls and correspondence, extra fares. You should keep a record of all these expenses as you go along.

split trial

The two elements of liability and of quantum (how much) can be decided separately if the plaintiff's solicitor, when starting proceedings, applies for there to be a split trial. This makes it possible for the question of liability to be dealt with first, while the events are likely to be still relatively fresh in everybody's memory. If liability is not proved, no further claim can then be made on the defendant.

If he is found liable, the question of how much shall be paid out is not decided at this hearing. When the longer term effects of the accident can be assessed, it is up to the plaintiff then to pursue proceedings for claiming damages.

The drawback of a split trial is the expense of two hearings; it may also be a disadvantage that a different person will be judging the two issues – perhaps one less favourable to the plaintiff's case at the second round than he who held the defendant to have been negligent in the first place. The advantage is that once liability is settled, negotiations as to quantum are likely to succeed and a second hearing may be avoided.

In Scotland, split trials are competent in the Court of Session but not in the sheriff court. They are hardly ever used.

interim payment

Where the extent of the injury and its long-term effects cannot yet be determined but the plaintiff needs extra finances to cope meanwhile, it is possible to ask for an interim payment during the early part of proceedings or negotiations, or after the first stage of a split trial. This payment is 'on account' to help with immediate expenses due to the injury and will be deducted when the assessment is finally made of the overall compensation due to the plaintiff.

The court can only award interim damages where

○ there is no dispute as to liability or the court is satisfied on a balance of probabilities that the plaintiff will at the trial obtain substantial damages against the defendant, *and*

○ the defendant is insured against the plaintiff's claim, or is a public authority or a person of substantial means and resources.

An interim payment will have to be repaid if the court eventually assesses the total award due at a lower figure, or none is payable at all because the defendant is found not liable after all, or contributory negligence consumes or reduces any award below the level of the interim payment.

A request for interim payment is usually for an item of special damages, to meet an actual expense, such as a wheelchair or other equipment to help with a disability.

An interim payment can be arranged between the parties. For example, an insurance company may voluntarily pay for an operation at an early stage, where this will speed recovery and thus lessen damages. Details are not given to the judge and the payment must not be referred to in further proceedings.

A large interim payment should not deter you from pursuing your claim for an appropriate overall sum – but the final award you get will be reduced by the amount you have already received (and probably already spent).

in Scotland

The court may award you interim damages if

○ the defender admits liability, *or*
○ the court is satisfied that you will establish the defender's liability and that you were not negligent to a substantial extent.

Interim damages can only be awarded if your action is defended. If it is undefended, you will be awarded the full amount of your claim in a few weeks' time.

provisional damages

Under normal personal injury litigation, a final judgment for damages extinguishes any possible grounds for asking for a further payment at any time if a worse condition develops from the same accident later on.

However, there is now (since 1 July 1985) a procedure for getting payment in two distinct stages: an initial 'provisional' payment with the option to apply for another payment at some future moment should a predicted disability occur or worsen.

A request for the case to be dealt with on a 'provisional damages' basis has to be made by the plaintiff's solicitor right at the beginning of proceedings as part of the particulars or statement of claim. (The defendant can contest the plaintiff's application.) It is a matter for the court to decide, on the merits of the case, whether the case should be dealt with on a provisional damages basis.

The statutory requirements are that the future condition will be 'serious' and that there is a 'chance' that it may develop – neither term being precisely defined judicially. The justification for making use of this procedure must be a medical specialist's considered opinion, that, on the basis of past experiences of similar conditions and circumstances, there is a chance, not a foreseeable probability, of a stated disease or disability occurring, and that it will have very serious additional consequences. For instance, the uninjured eye might develop sympathetic ophthalmia and lead to complete blindness, or severe mental deterioration arise after a head injury. Epilepsy, cancer, deafness, spinal curvature or paralysis, blood disease, have also been cited as potential conditions for a provisional damages claim.

When a 'provisional damages' case comes to court, the court decides liability and awards immediate damages in the normal way (without account of the 'chance' condition that might otherwise be included in the damages as a foreseeable event). If there has been a settlement out of court, the negotiated terms must be brought to the court for approval and for a provisional 'consent' judgment to be issued.

The court order will be that if a specified condition (the 'feared event') arises within a specified period of time, the plaintiff can come back to court to ask for a further award. More than one 'feared event' can be specified, each with its own time limit. It is possible to ask for an extension of the first time period, provided this is asked for within the existing time limit, if there seems still to be a chance that worse is yet to come. Otherwise, once the set period for a claim has expired, no further action can be brought.

the further claim
If, during the specified time, the anticipated condition makes its appearance to a serious extent, the proceedings can be re-opened by issuing a notice of intention to apply for further damages. The further damages can be settled by negotiation out of court, provided notice is given to the other party within the specified time limit. The court should be notified when this happens.

Since all this may be happening some years after the original claim, the people concerned may then be different and new to the case – solicitor, consultant, insurance officials, as well as the judge or master who hears your claim for these further damages. During the intervening period, you would be well advised to keep in touch with the solicitor and doctor(s), to report on your state of health or disability and to prevent the case 'going to sleep', as lawyers say. Remember especially to contact a solicitor and medical advisers about 6 months before the end of the time limit set by the court.

Any legal and medical costs incurred for monitoring purposes meanwhile will have to be met by you, as the plaintiff. The defendant could be ordered to repay these if a further damages claim succeeds.

If you were previously on legal aid, a fresh application for a certificate will have to be made. Whereas the merits of your case may not be in doubt, your financial circumstances if you received a large provisional award may now make you ineligible for a legal aid certificate.

The defendant may offer you a payment in settlement during the interim period, even if there are no signs of the specified deterioration, merely in order to close the matter and avoid the risk of a heavier payment in the future. You should consider very carefully before accepting such an offer. It would disentitle you from any further claim if your condition does seriously deteriorate later on.

provisional damages in Scotland

The statutory requirements are that there is a 'risk' that a serious disease or deterioration will develop in the future. The court need not set a time limit for the condition to develop in.

You apply for a further award by lodging a document (called a minute) which sets out your claims and outlines the supporting evidence. This minute is served on the defender who can lodge a document answering your claim. After a period for adjustment of the minute and answers, a date is set for the hearing.

payment when damages awarded

It is essential at the final settlement stage to have calculated all the expenses and losses, with documents in support, that you can possibly need to have reimbursed and to have prepared your claims in full. You cannot go back to ask for more if you later realise there was another aspect for which you could have claimed, or if an unforeseen reaction to an injury develops.

How much compensation you are to be paid for general damages will be decided on the basis of the factors you claim to have suffered or lost.

Although it may take years before you receive compensation through the court system, inflation is taken into account by the fact that an award for general damages is based on the value at the time of the court's decision, rather than as at the time the injury was sustained.

The court will see whether all the losses you claim as special damages are justified or have been agreed, and will order payment accordingly.

deductions for state payments
When a payment for special damages includes compensation for loss of earnings, a deduction will be made from it for any state payments that you have received in lieu of wages (such as statutory sick pay).

When you qualify for state benefits because of the long-term effects of your injury (for example, sickness benefit, invalidity benefit, severe disablement benefit), half of the amounts (whether already received or likely to be during a 5-year period from the date of the accident) will be deducted from your claim.

interest
Interest is added to the amounts payable to you, where appropriate. An award of interest is at the court's discretion, and can be refused.

Should you receive compensation for the loss of a career or for future earnings, no interest can be claimed because you are being paid this money, in effect, in advance.

Interest is payable to the date of judgment or settlement if that was earlier. In the High Court, an order can be issued to enforce the judgment debt; interest is then payable until the actual date of payment.

In personal injury claims, the interest rate on a claim for pain and suffering and loss of amenity under general damages is 2%. On special damages, interest is usually half the normal judgment debt rate (currently 15%) but it can be the full rate if specifically pleaded and the whole of the amount of special damages was incurred at an early stage – that is, soon after the accident.

in Scotland

In awarding damages, it is up to the court to decide how much to add on as representing interest. The normal pattern is to award interest at half the legal rate (currently 15%) from the date of the accident for past loss of earnings. The rate for solatium is usually higher.

The total sum awarded by the court (damages and interest) bears interest at the full legal rate from the date of the award until it is paid.

getting the payment

If your opponent was insured, or is a public authority or company, you should get a lump sum in total payment straight away. Where your opponent is an uninsured individual or a private company or business, it may not be possible for full payment to be made in one go and the court may order the lump sum to be paid by (specified) instalments. Should these fail to materialise, you should go back to the court to initiate enforcement – not always an easy or successful process.

Where agreement has been reached between you and your opponent without the case going to a court hearing, the arrangements for payment have to be made between yourselves, including payment of the legal costs and interest. There is no need to conclude with a formal court order 'by consent' (unless the plaintiff is a minor), but some insurers insist on it. There should at least be open correspondence which confirms that the payment that is made at the end is in full and final settlement.

in Scotland

What sum you get for solatium depends on how much you claimed and what the court thinks is fair. You will never be awarded more than you claim.

Except in summary cause procedure (for claims of not more than £1,000), the court has no power to award payment by instalments. It may, however, delay payment for a few months to allow the defender time to find the money.

If the defender does not pay, you can instruct the appropriate legal measures (called diligence) against the defender's property. You do not have to go back to court to do this.

unrecovered damages

Some household contents policies and personal liability policies provide insurance for 'reverse liability'.

If you obtained a court judgment in your favour which the person who was found liable cannot pay (because he is not insured or is a 'man of straw'), your own insurers will pay you the damages awarded to you if these have not been paid to you within three months of the date of the award.

This payment will only be made if the liability section of the policy would have insured you had the award been made against you rather than in your favour – the reverse situation.

The most you will get, whatever the outstanding debt, is usually the limit for the personal liability section of the policy (perhaps £500,000).

ACCIDENT WHERE THERE IS NO INJURY

In a case where there is no personal injury and the claim is a relatively straightforward one for damage to property resulting from the accident, you may feel in a position to commence proceedings and if necessary take the matter to court yourself. The Consumer Publication *Taking your own case to court or tribunal* sets out the procedure for taking a claim through the court.

You should first of all assemble your evidence and satisfy yourself that you can establish liability on the other party and that you have evidence supporting the amount you claim for damages.

Before commencing any court proceedings, write a 'letter before action' to the other party – the individual or the authority concerned. You should write without delay, alleging liability and what leads you to allege liability. If no satisfactory response, send a further letter warning of court proceedings if the claim is not settled within, say, 14 days.

Make sure that you keep a copy of any letters you write and, whenever writing, bear in mind that your letter may eventually be part of the evidence that is read to the court and it should therefore be couched in appropriate terms. Keep it simple – and courteous.

If the case is unlikely to result in the payment of compensation of less than £5,000, the proceedings should be commenced in the local county court. If likely to result in payment of more than £5,000 or if there is any doubt on the matter, proceedings should be commenced in the High Court. But if proceedings are required in the High Court, you should be instructing a solicitor: it is not advisable for a litigant-in-person to take on a High Court action.

Court proceedings should never be embarked on lightly. You must ensure that your evidence will support your claim and that you do have a good and valid claim for a reasonable sum. If you go to court unprepared and are unable to support your claim when you get there on the day, you will be seen to be wasting the court's time and if you were to lose, you would probably be ordered to pay the other party's costs. This can be a heavy burden if your opponent instructed a solicitor (which is very likely).

arbitration

If your claim is for less than £500, the case is normally heard by a county court registrar under the arbitration process. Even where the claim is for more than £500, it can be heard by arbitration if both parties agree or the registrar orders a referral to arbitration.

Arbitration is designed to be quicker and less formal than court cases generally are: the hearing is in private, the strict rules of evidence do not apply and the arbitrator (the registrar) who hears the case can decide on the way in which the case should proceed. He will do his best to put at ease anybody who is unrepresented by a solicitor. Be prepared for the defendant to be represented by solicitors, even if you are not.

With arbitration, solicitors' costs are not awarded, but if you are successful, you can claim reimbursement for some of your expenses including the court fees.

in Scotland

If your claim is for £500 or less, you must bring your action in the sheriff court. In other cases, there is a choice between the sheriff court and the Court of Session.

Claims not exceeding £1,000 in the sheriff court are dealt with under the relatively simple summary cause procedure. Above £1,000, the more complex ordinary procedure has to be used.

You might be able to pursue your claim under summary cause procedure yourself, although you would probably get out of your depth if the case was defended. You would be well advised not to attempt sheriff court ordinary procedure or any Court of Session litigation yourself.

Arbitration by court officials is not available in Scotland. At present, however small your claim is, you have to go through the appropriate court procedure.

ACCIDENT ON THE ROAD

The Association of British Insurers has issued a leaflet *Crunch! what to do next*, and the British Insurance Brokers' Association has issued *Car accident: your glove-pocket guide*, either of which could be useful to have in the car to refer to if you should be involved in a motoring accident. Some insurance companies supply their policyholders with a standard notice specifying what should and should not be done when there has been an accident.

Ideally, you keep a notepad and pen or pencil always in the car.

In a *Which?* report, the following advice was given on what to do if you have a car accident:

> After an accident, your first priority must be the safety and care of people involved. Obviously injuries need urgent attention. But remember that people who claim to be unhurt – and that goes for you, too – may still need treatment for shock, at least. And other traffic may need warning or control to avoid a worse pile-up. When that's taken care of, you can think about the legal side and insurance aspects.

1 STOP

You must, by law, stop and stay for a reasonable time if:

○ anyone else has been hurt
○ any roadside property or vehicle apart from your own has been damaged
○ any dog, sheep, cattle, horse, pig, donkey, mule or goat has been injured.

You must, by law, give your name and address to anyone involved in or affected by the accident if they ask for these details. If you haven't given your name and address to anyone, you must report the accident to the police within 24 hours.

2 WRITE DOWN

○ names, addresses and phone numbers of any independent witnesses – as many as possible
○ the registration number of any car whose occupants may have seen what happened
○ the date and time the accident happened.

3 GET THE OTHER DRIVER'S

○ name
○ address
○ phone number
○ insurance company (the other driver doesn't have to tell you this if no one is injured)
○ make of car
○ registration number of car.

4 DON'T DISCUSS WHAT HAPPENED

and don't admit liability, apologise or offer any payment even if you think the accident was your fault.

5 CALL THE POLICE IF

○ anyone is injured, or
○ you think the other driver has committed an offence, or
○ you've damaged someone else's property and can't find them to tell, or
○ you're certain you're not to blame (though the police may not want to know).

6 WRITE DOWN WHAT HAPPENED, NOTING

○ any injury to people, or damage to vehicles and other property
○ the state of traffic (e.g. heavy, fast moving)
○ weather conditions and visibility
○ road surface conditions
○ any signals which were being made by you or anyone else
○ colour of other vehicles involved, how roadworthy they were, whether they had lights on

○ identity numbers of policemen
○ what other people said
○ what you said (hopefully, nothing incriminating).

Keep your on-the-spot notes even if you make a fair copy.

7 MAKE A SKETCH MAP, INDICATING THE EXACT LOCATION AND MARK ON IT

○ approximate road speeds, and direction of travel, of everybody concerned
○ position of cars immediately before and after the accident, and distances they were from each other, from road junctions, and from the side of the road
○ positions and lengths of skid marks
○ names, widths and gradients of roads
○ position of any witnesses
○ any traffic signs or road markings
○ any obstructions to the view of the traffic (e.g. sharp bend, brick wall, hedge, parked car)
○ which way is north.

Try to protect the scene by preventing other road users from crashing into it. This should be done by encouraging bystanders to wave down the traffic, remembering to send them some distance from the scene, particularly if it is situated near a bend or over the brow of a hill.

If you happen to have a camera with you, take photographs of the scene of the accident and any damage before the vehicles are moved, particularly if the police do not come and carry out a detailed investigation.

On the sketch map show the points from which your photographs were taken.

the other driver
If you can possibly avoid it, do not discuss the details of the accident with the other driver. Do not admit it was your fault (even if you think it was) and try not to apologise for what happened. An admission of blame or an apology may preju-

dice your right to recover under your insurance policy. In fact, say as little as possible.

You should make a note there and then of what the other driver (or anyone else) says: for instance, some excuse for the state of his vehicle or blaming some external condition for the accident. Even if not an admission of liability, it shows that he is placing the blame for the accident on some factor other than you. Should he apologise or offer to pay for your damage or anything of that nature, write down what he says as precisely as possible.

Even if the other driver fails to stop, you should note as many circumstances as possible about the incident. If you or any witness were able to note the registration number of the vehicle, you would stand a good chance of discovering who is the legal 'keeper' of the vehicle, through the police. You would also have to do this if you find out afterwards that the other driver gave a false name and address.

when someone is injured

It would be wise to keep a sensible first-aid book in the car, such as the British Red Cross Society's booklet *Motorists' first aid* (Dorling Kindersley, £1.95) which gives step-by-step illustrations of emergency care for road users. Then you, or someone else at the scene, can provide the correct immediate treatment for any injury. Unless you have specialist medical knowledge, do not move anybody who is badly injured or unconscious: you may do more harm than good. Send for an ambulance at once. There is no charge for an emergency '999' call.

There is a voluntary organisation – the British Association for Immediate Care (BASICS) – of doctors who come to the scene of an accident in specially equipped cars when alerted by the police or the ambulance service. A BASICS team works with ambulancemen to give specialised immediate treatment to an injured person during the time between the accident and getting to hospital, to stabilise the casualty's condition and prevent complications before reaching hospital. This service is particularly vital in rural areas where the time between injury and hospital treatment is likely to be prolonged. (BASICS is administered from 31c Lower Brook Street, Ipswich, Suffolk IP4 1AQ.)

the police

You must call the police when someone has been injured. This may mean getting to a telephone, or asking someone else, to ring the nearest police station via '999'.

While waiting for the police to come, try to jot down some notes (instead of indulging in recriminations with the other driver). This may calm you down, and nobody can later claim that you delayed unreasonably in making notes.

As soon as the police officers arrive, find out what police station they have come from and write this down, and also the identification number of each policeman (this is on the shoulder of his jacket) and/or ask his name.

Once the police arrive, the matter will be out of your hands to a large extent. Their investigations may involve checking your car to find out whether all parts of it comply fully with the relevant statutory requirements. You may be asked to produce appropriate documents, such as insurance certificate, driving licence, MoT certificate, if not there and then, within a stipulated time at a police station.

The police may ask you and any other driver involved in the accident to take a breathalyser test, in case either of you has been drinking. It is a criminal offence to refuse a police request for a breath test (or a urine test, if taken to the police station) unless you have a 'reasonable' excuse – and acceptable excuses are few and far between.

A policeman will ask each person who was involved in the accident or who witnessed it to give their name and address. He may ask each of them to tell his or her version of what happened or will get a statement from them later.

If the police consider that anyone has committed an offence, they will caution the person by saying that he is not obliged to say anything, but that anything he does say will be taken down in writing and may be used in evidence at a later stage. If you decide not to say anything at the time, you do not have to do more than give your name and address. You may be too shaken to be thinking clearly at that stage and it would be wise not to make a statement until later on when you have had time to think and seek advice. If you want to speak to your solicitor before making a statement, you are entitled to say that you want to do this.

police report
A copy of the report prepared by the police after an accident can be obtained in due course from the appropriate police station for a fee (currently £27 for a request for a full report, £12 for a minor or partial report).

A police report sets out the drivers' names, addresses, car registration numbers, the insurers. It will give the names and addresses of any witnesses interviewed by the police and some of their statements. The report will also include details of the road conditions, visibility, whether street lighting was on, whether seatbelts were worn, and, briefly, what injuries were suffered and what property damaged. There will also be a statement from the police officer(s) who attended, and probably a sketch plan of the site.

The police report can be an important document for establishing liability. It will not, however, be released to you while criminal proceedings are being contemplated or taken against any of the parties involved in the incident. In such a case, you will have to contact the police station to find out what is happening. If the defendant is convicted of a motoring offence, ask the clerk of the magistrates' court for a certificate of conviction because this is some evidence of the other person's negligence.

Even where a police report has been prepared, this may not provide sufficient detail about what happened to support your claim for damages. The police are concerned with discovering whether an offence has been committed and deciding whether to prosecute, whereas you are concerned with apportioning blame as the basis for a claim for damages.

charges for medical treatment

A particular feature of a road accident where someone is injured is that the law imposes charges for emergency national health service medical treatment. (These charges, which are laid down by statute and reviewed every year, are covered by motor insurance policies.)

A doctor who gives immediate roadside treatment to someone injured as a result of a motor accident can therefore charge the person who was using the car at the time, an emergency treatment fee of £14.19, plus a 28p mileage allowance if he comes more than 2 miles to get to the scene.

Also a fee is payable for hospital treatment: the maximum is currently £1,892.50 for inpatient treatment, £189.25 for out-patient treatment. These charges are in accordance with the Road Traffic Acts and have to be paid even where the motorist is totally innocent.

The hospital where the treatment is given will send an account to the home address of the patient, with a printed sheet explaining briefly this part of the Road Traffic Act. When such a claim is sent to you, pass it immediately to your insurance company with a request to pay; this does not imply any admission of liability. Acknowledge receipt of the account to the area health authority, giving them the name and address of your insurers and the policy and claim numbers.

claiming on insurance when someone is injured

You and the driver of the other vehicle must tell each other the names of your insurers.

Your own motor insurance policy will cover your legal liability for injuries to anyone else – your passengers, another driver, his passengers, pedestrians or other road users. There is no financial limit to such cover, and your insurers will handle on your behalf the claim of any injured person.

Any passenger who is injured will have the right to claim on the driver(s), whose insurance has to cover such a third party claim provided the driver was 'negligent'. This means that a wife can claim on her husband for damages if he was the driver and was negligent (and vice versa) and children on their parent.

If the victim is an innocent bystander, he or she can recover damages from any of the drivers at fault, or all of them collectively. It is unlikely that the claim will be settled until there is agreement between the drivers as to each one's share of responsibility. There is often a formal agreement between motor insurers ('the third party sharing agreement') which, subject to certain quite high monetary limits, provides that the insurers will share the claims of innocent victims equally, irrespective of degrees of fault of the respective drivers.

when you are injured
An injured policyholder cannot claim on his own policy for damages for himself. Most 'comprehensive' motor policies, however, provide for one lump sum payment (£5,000 perhaps or only £1,000) to the policyholder if he should lose the sight of one eye or the use of a limb due to the accident. There is an upper age limit of 70 with some policies: anyone older than that at the time of the accident gets nothing.

So, if you are injured while driving your own car, you have to claim on the party who can be held responsible for the accident, submitting medical and other evidence in support. Motorists must, by law, be insured for this liability so your claim will be passed to the other driver's insurers and you have to achieve compensation from them.

You would be wise to seek advice from a solicitor experienced in handling injury compensation claims, or your motoring organisation or trade union representative. A claim for compensation for bodily injury is not a do-it-yourself exercise. Even if it is clear whose fault it was and that compensation is due on a 100 per cent liability basis, someone who is not knowledgeable about law or insurance cannot possibly know how much money to ask for or expect to receive.

victim of uninsured or untraced motorist

If the other driver proves untraceable or was uninsured, a claim for compensation for bodily injuries suffered in a road traffic accident (and loss of wages as a result of the injuries) can be made to the Motor Insurers' Bureau.

The MIB, a company formed and funded by motor insurers, has agreements with the government to provide compensation for victims of uninsured or untraced drivers who have sustained bodily injury.

To claim compensation from the MIB under the uninsured drivers' agreement, you must notify the Bureau before you start legal proceedings against the uninsured driver or within 7 days of issuing proceedings. If the driver at fault has a motor policy but, for some reason, it does not apply, the insurers of that policy will usually deal with the claim, as agent for the MIB. If there is no policy involved, the MIB will appoint an insurer to deal with the matter on their behalf. In either case, the claim will be handled only to the extent that the uninsured motorist is legally liable and then only if there is no other party who may also be liable.

After a 'hit-and-run' accident where the driver cannot be traced, you must apply direct to the MIB within three years of the accident. You will be sent a form to complete, requiring full details of your injuries, the circumstances of the accident, your occupation, and authorising the MIB to approach your employers, your doctor, the hospital, government departments, insurers, for any information relevant to your application.

The address of the Motor Insurers' Bureau is New Garden House, 78 Hatton Garden, London EC1N 8JQ (telephone 01-242 0033).

seatbelts

It is obligatory for front seat passengers as well as drivers to wear a seatbelt (only in rare cases is exemption granted).

As well as the penalty imposed if you disobey this requirement of the law, you may also find that your claim on the other driver for damages for any injuries suffered may be reduced if the injuries might have been avoided or lessened had you been wearing a seatbelt. The reduction because of your contributory negligence may be between 15 and 25 per cent of that part of the damages which relates to injuries that might have been avoided or reduced had seatbelts been in use. Seatbelts can often reduce serious injuries but can themselves tend to cause other injuries so, as a general rule of thumb, there is a 20 per cent reduction. But if the court is satisfied that no injuries would have been incurred had you been wearing a seatbelt, no compensation at all would be given.

accident investigators

There are firms of specialist investigators (consulting engineers, ex-policemen) who can be called in to ascertain exactly what did happen. They do this by visits to the scene, examining vehicles, taking photographs, measurements and observations, scale plans, reference to police notes taken at the time which may not have been analysed if prosecution did not follow, position of bodies, with computerised analysis of the data.

Accident investigators interpret the physical evidence to establish speeds and the likely movements of the vehicles before the collision. Mathematical analysis may be possible based on movement of vehicles after impact, tyre marks, position and extent of damage, nature of injuries. An investigator may also interview hospital doctors and other specialists to get an independent opinion of injuries and long-term disability.

An accident investigation firm can be brought in by insurers or by solicitors or by an individual. Their professional evidence may carry a lot of weight at a court hearing or during negotiations about liability. The fees for such an investigation vary according to the complexity of the circumstances and the extent of the report required by the client.

'ambulance chaser'

Another type of 'investigator' is a person or a firm, who suggests – usually when you are in a distressed or emotional state as a result of the accident – that you authorise them to act on your behalf for a high rate of commission. Their interest is in settling the claim quickly and getting their percentage, regardless of whether they get a fair and adequate settlement for you. Do not let an 'ambulance chaser' handle your case.

damaged vehicle

At the time of the impact, it may not be apparent how much damage has been caused to your car and therefore how much you are going to want to claim from the other person. It is important to examine both vehicles as carefully as possible: apparently superficial damage to a bumper may conceal more serious damage to the bodywork below. Many disputes come to court solely because the driver responsible for the accident did not realise the seriousness of the damage done. It is worth making as detailed a note as possible about the damage to each vehicle. Photographs taken as soon after the accident as possible – even if only of your own vehicle – can be invaluable.

Although there is no requirement to call the police where nobody has been injured, if there has been a lot of damage or the other driver is creating difficulties – or has cleared off – it would be advisable to ask the police to come. It can also be helpful to have the police come where damage has been caused to another person's property – a wall or fence, perhaps, windows or a garden shed.

Many people think that the law requires drivers to have full third party insurance. But there is no legal requirement for insurance for a driver's liability for damage to property; at present, the law says only that drivers must have insurance for their liability for injuries caused to other people. This means that the arrangements applying to claims in respect of damage to property are different in some respects from those governing the conduct of personal injury claims arising out of road accidents.

claiming on insurance

Whatever the circumstances of an accident with another car when you are driving, you should at all times be aware of what insurance cover applies – and act in accordance with the policy conditions: check time limits and procedures as soon as you can after the event, and adhere to them precisely.

As soon as possible, inform your insurers of the accident. This is a condition of your policy. Anyone whose insurance is with a Lloyds' syndicate should contact his broker.

Have a look at the 'Conditions' of your motor policy and you will see one or more clauses setting out what you have to do. There are minor variations, but the essential features of the notification clause are:

○ notice must be given in writing (this does not stop you telephoning, but you must write as well)
○ this written notice must give full particulars of the occurrence
○ it must be sent to the insurers as soon as possible after the occurrence.

You must comply even if you do not intend to make a claim on your own motor policy. A simple notification does not risk your no-claim discount (NCD).

Confirm any telephone conversation with a follow-up letter, giving the date of the accident, quoting your policy number and asking for an accident report form or a claim form.

not claiming
If you do not intend to make a claim, mark the accident report form clearly 'for information only' or tick a box on the form to indicate this, so that your no-claim discount is not affected. But if you decide not to make a claim on your own policy, you cannot go back to your insurers later, after you have got into difficulties in making your own claim or because a claim is made against you, telling them you have changed your mind. They will not then accept your claim. So, think carefully before deciding not to make a claim on your own policy. And if anyone has been injured in the accident, you would be foolish not to invoke your own motor policy.

Bear in mind that if, for whatever reason, you do not want to claim on your policy for the damage to your own vehicle, the other driver may consider the accident your fault and take court action against you – perhaps months or even years later. If you have not reported the accident promptly, your insurers will refuse to indemnify you or to cover the cost of court proceedings.

other driver at fault?
If you are sure that the other driver was at fault and you do not want to make a claim on your own policy so as to preserve a good no-claim discount or because you have a large 'excess' on your policy (when you have yourself to pay £xxx of any claim), you may want to claim on the other motorist.

Or if your own policy is limited to third party claims and fire and theft, or is only the basic Road Traffic Act cover, and you want to get payment for the cost of repairs to your own car, you would have to claim from the other motorist. Also, even if yours is a 'comprehensive' policy, there may be items of expense that are not covered which you could claim from the other person and more compensation for your injuries.

It is essential to be aware of the fundamental difference in your rights against the other party's insurers and your relationship with your own insurers. In theory, there would seem to be little difference whether you claim on your own policy or via the other motorist's policy, particularly if the same company happens to be insuring both of you. In practice, this is far from the truth.

If you claim on the other motorist, you are in an adversarial situation. You are the 'third party' so far as the other person's insurers are concerned: you are asserting that their policyholder has some legal liability to compensate you and your right to compensation depends on the complex rules of liability (establishing duty of care, breach of duty, negligence causing loss). His insurers will examine each facet of the claim that you make, in order to decide whether or not their policyholder has, in law, any obligation to compensate you.

If you have an accident causing only damage to property, all the law requires is that the motorists involved exchange their own names and addresses: you are not entitled to be given details of the other motorist's insurance (unlike the situation where there has been a personal injury). If he does not volunteer the information, you can only hope that he will either pass your claim on to his insurers to deal with or agree to pay up himself.

If he passes on your claim but his insurers consider that their policyholder was not responsible for the accident, they will repudiate your claim. The criterion is whether you have a valid claim in law against him, that is, whether you can prove that the other driver's negligence in some way caused, or contributed to, the accident.

Your opponent may have decided not to invoke his own policy. If that be the case then, even if you know the name of his insurers, they will not deal with your claim: legally they have no authority from their insured so to do.

making a third-party claim

Provided that you are able to prove that the other party can be held liable for the damage caused, items you could claim for include

○ roadside repairs
○ towing by breakdown van to repairers' garage
○ storage charges at repairers
○ cost of repairs or write-off value of car
○ damage to or loss of contents of car
○ loss of use of car and/or
○ hire of alternative car and/or
○ travel expenses (bus fares etc) while your car is being repaired
○ loss of your no-claim discount
○ reduced value of repaired car.

You should give the other party or his insurers the opportunity to inspect the damage before the repairs are carried out. This is an instance of the difference between a claim involving another motorist's insurers and claiming on your own insurance. When your own insurers send an engineer along to inspect, provided he is satisfied that the work proposed is necessary, he can tell the repairers to go ahead and submit the bill to them. Where the other motorist's insurers are involved, they never give instructions to the repairers on your behalf.

You would have to show that any expenses and claims were reasonable under the circumstances and that you had not failed to 'mitigate' your loss – that is, you endeavoured to keep your expenses down to a reasonable level.

loss of use of car

If your damaged car is no longer driveable, you may need to have a replacement car while your own is off the road. If you decide to hire a car in the hope that the other driver, or his insurers, will pay for the cost, keep all the hiring accounts so that you can produce them to prove the amount you have spent on car hire. (But remember – hire cars are expensive, so do not incur heavy bills if the other driver is, or may be, uninsured.)

A basic legal principle applies: you cannot expect the other person, even if he is fully responsible for your misfortune, to put you in a better position than you were before his act or omission. So, you can claim only for the cost of hiring a car in a similar category to your own – not, for example, a D registration BMW when yours is an A registration Ford Escort.

Suppose that you decide to do without a car temporarily because there is sufficient public transport locally for your needs. You should keep an accurate note of your journeys and your expenditure day-to-day so that you can provide sufficient detail when you come to put in your claim for 'loss of use' expenses. These should also include for other members of your household having to pay out on fares because you cannot drive them around.

Whether you hire a car or pay to travel by public or private transport, the other insurers may deduct from your claim the normal costs of running your car, which you would have incurred over the period. This is another application of the insurance rule that you cannot profit out of the incident: you should be no worse off, but no better off, than you would have been had the accident not occurred.

legal expenses insurance for claiming uninsured losses

Legal expenses cover added on to an existing comprehensive motor policy or a household policy will specifically include the expense of claiming 'uninsured losses' from another motorist. Cases which are covered by any other insurance policy are excluded.

The insurance only applies if you are using a solicitor (it exists mainly to cover his fees), and is designed primarily for cases that go to court, but it will cover the legal bills if you settle without the case going to court. A case already under way when you take out a policy will not be eligible.

The policy cannot be invoked after legal proceedings have already been started: you have to give the legal expenses insurers full details of the situation from the start. The insurers have the right to vet your choice of solicitor.

The insurers stipulate that they can make their own investigations into your case or try to negotiate a settlement on your behalf. They can refuse to cover a case if they consider that you do not have a reasonable chance of success or if the person against whom you wish to claim would not be able to pay you compensation.

third party claim on you

Your policy conditions include a clause detailing what you must do with letters and legal documents that you receive after an accident. It will tell you that every letter or claim and every summons, writ or other legal process must be sent to the insurers immediately.

If it should happen that you receive a letter blaming you for the accident, you must do what your insurers then tell you to do – unless you want to run the risk of their refusing you the protection of your policy when you most need it.

Send such a letter straight to your insurers, with your own account of the incident and any witness's statement. Thereafter, pass any further correspondence from the other party to your insurers, unanswered, taking a copy before you do so.

If it can be established that you were to blame for the accident, your insurers will pay the other person's claim. But unless you tell them to deal with the case, they will not, and he would then have to sue you to try to get the money.

making a claim on your own insurance

With 'comprehensive' insurance, you can claim on your own policy for the damage done to your car and damage caused by you to another's car or other property.

Send the claim form or accident report form to your insurers as soon as you have completed it, even if you do not yet have an estimate for the cost of repairs to your car.

You should let the insurers know where the damaged vehicle is. They may suggest that you take it to, or have it collected by, one of their recommended repairers but you are not obliged to do this unless it is a policy condition. If the car is immobilised as a result of the accident and has to be towed to a garage or repairer, you can include in your claim the cost of towing.

You must ask for an estimate for the repairs. Normally, an estimate is sent to you to pass on to your insurers.

Check with your insurers what you should do about authorising the repairs to be done. You may find that there is a figure laid down in your policy below which you can yourself give instructions to the garage to start the work. Otherwise, you should give the insurers reasonable time to arrange for their engineer to inspect the car at the repairers' premises before work is started. Usually, the engineer is someone employed by the insurers; some insurers, mainly Lloyds' syndicates, use independent firms of motor claims assessors.

Once the engineer is satisfied that the car is repairable and agrees the estimate with the repairer, he authorises the repairs to be carried out, and sends his report to the insurers.

betterment

The insurers will tell you whether there are any items which the insurance does not cover and for which you may be asked to pay yourself.

If it is considered that the parts that are to be replaced were already worn, damaged or rusted prior to the accident, you may be required to pay a proportion of their replacement cost for 'betterment' – because the car will come back to you better than it was before the accident. If a wing of your car was damaged but was already about to disintegrate due to rust, it would obviously be impractical and pointless to replace a rusty wing with another rusty one. But it would be unfair to expect the insurers to pay the whole cost of a new wing which you would probably have had to replace in due course anyway: the insurers are entitled to make a deduction to cover the improvement to your car.

Normally, insurance companies are reasonable about betterment and only claim a deduction where the part replaced was severely worn.

when the work is done

The cost of getting the car back to you is covered by most insurance policies, so if you have to go by train to collect it, you can claim the cost of a single fare.

If you have to pay any part of the bill yourself, because of betterment or an excess, you will have to pay this amount to the garage before you will be allowed to take the car away. The rest of the bill will be paid by the insurers to the garage direct or by reimbursement to you. The bill will have details of what was done to the car, so it is wise to ask for a copy of it to keep.

You are expected to inspect the car yourself and may be asked to sign a collection note or satisfaction note stating that the repairs have been carried out to your satisfaction. The repairers will send this to the insurers with their bill. If you signed a satisfaction note and the repairs turn out to be unsatisfactory, notify the insurers and the garage straight away and get the insurers to arrange with the garage for the further repair work to be carried out.

substitute car

You may be able to claim on your own insurance for the cost of hiring a substitute car or of alternative transport until you buy a new one (or while yours is being repaired). There may be a limit set in your policy on the number of weeks' hiring costs which will be reimbursed. Check this before you run up hiring bills over a longer period than your insurance will cover. Even if there is nothing specific in the policy, you will generally only be able to claim for the time it would take you to get your own car repaired if you acted promptly.

If you are told that your vehicle is a 'write-off', your right to claim hiring costs from your insurers does not stop straight away, but at the point when you have had a reasonable opportunity to find and buy another car – perhaps two to three weeks.

when the car is unrepairable

The engineer's report may recommend that, from the insurers' point of view, it is not an economic proposition to repair the car where the repairs would cost more than the pre-accident value of the car, unless the car has some special value (for example, a vintage car).

The insurers may write to the effect that, in their view, the pre-accident value (usually based on a publication known as *Glass's Guide*) is, say, £800, that the scrap value is £50 and that they will not agree to any repair costs in excess of £750. However strongly you feel about repairing and keeping that particular car, if it would cost the insurers less to pay you the total loss (or 'write-off') value than to pay for repairing it, you cannot insist on having the repairs paid for instead.

All you can do is to

○ seek to provide special reasons why this particular car should be repaired even at a price in excess of its market value (difficult)
○ obtain expert evidence from a motor assessor showing that the car is worth more than the figure given by the insurers
○ accept the total loss payment and pay the excess repair costs yourself.

total loss settlement

A total loss settlement is usually on the basis of the current market value of the car for the condition it was in immediately before the accident, or the sum insured – whichever is the less.

Your insurers are obliged to discharge any outstanding hire purchase debt on the car when agreeing a total loss settlement, so if there is such a debt only the balance of the settlement figure comes to you.

A total loss settlement is usually made on the basis that the insured agrees that the salvage will become the property of the insurers, for disposal.

example of a simple accident

You are driving at 30 mph along a suburban street which is intersected by a number of similar suburban streets with white lines at each intersection. Another motorist, ignoring the lines against him, ignoring the give-way sign on his approach to this particular crossroads, drives out into your path from the nearside road. There is a collision, both cars sustain damage – yours to the front and near side – but fortunately no one is injured.

As the law requires, you exchange names and addresses, and so you learn that the other motorist is Jack Jones of 25 High Street, Surburbiton, but not whether he is the owner (and therefore the holder of a motor insurance policy) or someone using the car with the owner's permission or on the owner's business. You have to ask him – and he does have to tell you who the owner is and the owner's address. Having complied with the law, he is entitled without more ado to drive off (if his car is still driveable). But Jack Jones is a reasonable, decent chap, even if he has just (in your view) caused an accident. He tells you that he owns the car, gives you his full name and address and says that he will report the accident to his insurers.

At the scene of the collision, you note as accurately as you can where your car was at the moment of impact and where it finally came to rest. You also note the position of skid marks, the position of broken glass, plastic or metal from either car, the condition of the road, other traffic and the time of day.

Even as you are getting out of the car to speak with Jack Jones, you look around to see if there are any passers-by who saw what happened – pedestrians, cyclists, motorists – or any people in nearby gardens, clipping their hedges or whatever. You knew that it was important to get names and addresses before these people disappear or decide that they do not want to be involved.

Quite a lot to do in a moment of stress, but you have kept calm, and have collected your evidence.

example **107**

You needed to get a breakdown van to tow the car to a suitable repairers where an estimate is being prepared, and you made a note of the cost of this and the name of the breakdown firm.

You want an estimate prepared with all reasonable speed, whether you are going to get Jack Jones to pay or his insurers, or your insurers, and even if you have to meet part or all of the cost yourself. Because of the extent of the damage, this may take the repairers a day or two to prepare – they may have to strip down the clearly damaged parts to see whether anything else is wrong.

You decide not to invoke your own insurance because you consider the accident to have been entirely Jack Jones' fault, and to take on the hassle of the claim yourself. You merely inform your insurers that the accident has happened.

You begin by writing to Jack Jones, a short, straightforward letter to be sent by recorded delivery:

Dear Mr Jones

I am writing concerning the collision between our cars at the East Street/North Street crossroads at noon today. I hold you fully responsible for the collision and for the damage to my Ford Escort A123 PQR. An estimate for the repairs is being prepared by Main Street Motors and I will send this to you in a day or so. The cost of the repairs is likely to be in excess of £250 and my car will be off the road for about a fortnight once instructions are given for the repairs to be done. As I cannot now use my car, I shall be claiming for its loss of use as well as for the cost of repairs.

I suggest that you pass this letter to your insurers straight away (in compliance with the claims conditions in your policy) and ask them to get in touch with me as soon as possible and arrange to inspect my car.

Yours truly

That and no more: the phrase "I hold you fully responsible" is sufficiently indicative of your present intention. Keep a copy of your letter.

There is no obligation to get more than one estimate. But if the cost of repairs is disputed, it will help if you have obtained two at least. Both should be sent to the other driver. It is important to get estimates as quickly as possible.

When you get the estimate, you send another letter, also short and to the point:

Dear Mr Jones

Following my letter of   (*date*), I now enclose copy of the estimate from Main Street Motors for the repairs to my car A123 PQR for the sum of £325 plus VAT. Please pass this to your insurers. For their information, I shall delay giving instructions for the repairs to be carried out until 7 days from today's date, in case they wish to send their motor engineer to inspect my car at Main Street Motors, Main Street, Surburbiton. Thereafter, I shall instruct the repairs to be carried out without further delay.

Yours truly

Enclose a copy of the estimate, and keep a copy of your letter.

At all times, you are in Jack Jones' hands. If he does not pass your letters on to his insurers, there is nothing you can do to get at them, and his failure to comply with his claims conditions may put them even farther out of reach. Your only remedy then would be to take Jack Jones to court.

However, Jack Jones does pass your letters and the estimate to his insurers, and has told them his version of the accident. But his insurance company's claims department fails to contact you before your 7-day deadline is reached. You cannot wait indefinitely for the other insurers' engineer to inspect. You have a legal duty to minimize your damage even though you say the collision was not your fault. You cannot sit back for weeks with your car off the road; you must get the repairs carried out with all reasonable speed. If you do delay, you will find that when the repairs are eventually done, the other insurers will not pay your claim for the loss of use of the car for all those weeks, but only for the two or three weeks that they

example **109**

say would have been sufficient for the repairs to be carried out if instructions had been given expeditiously.

So, you grit your teeth and tell the repairers to get on with the work (payment for which will come to be your responsibility) and you document this with another letter (again, keeping a copy):

> Dear Mr Jones
>
> I have today given instructions for the repairs to my car, A123 PQR, to be carried out. The car will be at Main Street Motors, Surburbiton for approximately another fortnight.
>
> Yours truly

His insurers will be considering the circumstances of the accident as explained to them by him. If he merely informed them of the accident but did not invoke his policy by making a claim on it, he can instruct them to disregard your claim. But if he claims for repairs to his own car, he must leave it to his insurers to deal with your third party claim on him.

A day or two later comes a letter to you from the regional claims office of Universal Insurance plc, Jack Jones' insurance company. It is a standard all-purpose 'tick-box' letter, to the effect that the insurers do not admit liability on behalf of their insured but that they have instructed their staff engineer to inspect your car. They ask you to let them know the name, address and reference of your own insurers.

getting the repairs done and paid for

The Universal Insurance company follow this up with a further letter after their engineer has inspected the car. While still not admitting liability, they say that they accept the estimate as reasonable. This letter at least removes the worry that they may later dispute the amount of the bill.

(Very rarely do insurers admit liability at any stage on a third party's claim. An insurer who admits any liability on behalf of the insured without express consent could, in law, be held to be libelling or slandering the insured.)

When the repairs are complete, you have to pay the bill – and endeavour to recover the amount from Jack Jones or his insurers. Insurers usually do not pay the amount direct to the repairers when it is a third party claim.

You check that the bill lines up with the estimate. If there were discrepancies – perhaps because in the course of repair, other parts were found to have been damaged, or additional labour costs have been incurred – you would have to get a written explanation from the repairers why it is for a different sum or differs in detail from the estimate. You then send a copy of the repair bill to Jack Jones' insurance company (keeping the original).

evidence on liability

You must assemble evidence to show that Jack Jones was responsible for the accident and that his insurers should therefore pay out.

You write a polite, short letter to each witness, sending a stamped addressed envelope for their reply:

> Dear . . .
>
> I think you saw the collision between two cars at the East Street/North Street crossroads at noon on .... Can you please tell me in your own words, in as much detail as possible, what you saw. It will also help if you can say whether one motorist was to blame and, if so, which, or whether both were?
>
> I look forward to your early reply.
>
> Yours sincerely

Detailed questions need not be asked at this stage: these can come later if need be. And you are careful not to attempt to suggest to the witness what answer you expect – merely ask his opinion on responsibility, even though this may be adverse to your case.

example **111**

Witnesses may give you evidence of, say, high speed and sudden braking, or that Jack Jones, although travelling at a normal speed, was not keeping a proper look-out.

You need to have ready all the information you have collected when you come to argue with Universal Insurance over the degree of responsibility that Jack Jones had for the accident: a sketch of the crossroads, measurements, skid marks, positions of pieces of glass, plastic, metal from off the cars, together with the names and addresses of witnesses. But you do not give all this information to Universal yet. You have to decide how strong a hand you have. One important point in your favour against Jack Jones is the fact that he passed a give-way sign.

When you have built up your case, you write to Universal Insurance reaffirming that they must pay you, saying:

> "I have ample evidence to show that your policyholder was responsible for the collision. First of all, he passed a give-way sign without slowing down; secondly, I have the names and addresses of witnesses who say that he approached the crossroads at a high speed . . ."

the negotiation
Some insurers deal with this kind of claim by correspondence, in which case you may be in for a further exchange of letters before you get your money. Others send one of their claims inspectors to see you and try to agree an amount. Whichever course Universal choose to take, you must make up your mind whether you want 100 per cent or are prepared to accept something less. Remember that when two cars collide at crossroads, it is often the case that both motorists are in some degree to blame.

If you are dealing with your claim by correspondence, you have time to consider how best to deal with each letter and each argument. If you have a meeting with an insurance inspector, you may perhaps feel, or actually be, disadvantaged because he is an expert, well used to dealing with claimants such as yourself. Try to slow the discussion down to your own pace, do not concede points in argument unless the evidence is incontrovertible, try to reserve your position if you feel yourself to be under attack. You may want to have a reliable, firm friend with you to give you confidence.

settlement

Accepting an offer of less than 100 per cent of a claim is not an admission that the claimant is x% at fault, unless this is formally stated. If you settle for less than 100 per cent, you should ensure that the other driver's insurers acknowledge on his behalf that he has no further claim against you and that the sum paid is in full settlement of any claim that either driver may have.

Jack Jones' insurers offer you £350 "without prejudice, in full and final settlement" and you decide to accept this, after checking with your own insurers that this will not create any problems. An agreement to compromise without telling your own insurers what you are doing may create a situation where they may be unwilling to give you indemnity if a counterclaim is subsequently received from the third party.

disabled driver in an accident

The driver of a car with an orange badge, or the disabled passenger in the car, is unlikely to be able to get out of the car at the scene of an accident to exchange addresses, measure distances, take notes or catch possible witnesses before they fade away. If the driver is alone in his vehicle, he is completely dependent on the other motorist or his passengers or on the goodwill of any bystanders and will have to tell a would-be helper how best to help him.

If a wheelchair is being carried in the car for someone not normally ambulant, the chair may be damaged after a rear-end collision and may be unfit for use, immobilising the disabled person.

The loss of a wheelchair or walking aid, caliper or artificial limb, could increase the damages that a disabled person would need to claim. An artificial limb or a wheelchair supplied through an artificial limb and appliance centre (ALAC), run by the DHSS, will be replaced without cost, provided that it was not negligence on the owner's part that caused the damage. In most cases, a DHSS wheelchair can be replaced within a week or so, but a privately bought chair would have to be claimed for and could take a long time. Temporary replacement of a disabled person's damaged car may be impossible if the driver needs automatic transmission and/or special hand controls or other adaptations.

Time is needed to assess the residual disability of an injured person, particularly the effect of the new injury on an existing disability.

The inconvenience to a disabled person of the inordinate length of the time that it takes for a compensation claim to be settled is likely to be greater than for an able bodied person. Unless the disabled person is so affluent as to be able to replace an adapted car, for instance, and wait to be refunded years later when the claim is finally settled, it would be advisable to ask the solicitor to request an interim payment to cover necessary immediate payments. This can be done once the liability of the other party has been established sufficiently.

The disabled person may not have easy access, especially with a wheelchair, to official premises – police station, social security office, insurance company offices, or even to a solicitor's rooms – which adds to the inconvenience and difficulty of pursuing and enforcing a claim.

All these points should be included when quantifying the loss that the injured person has suffered.

accident not involving another driver

You may have an accident with your car that is not a collision with another vehicle. You may be forced to swerve and crash the car because, for instance, a pedestrian steps into the road unexpectedly, a bicyclist wobbles in front of you, a dog leaps down from a wall. If damage is done to your car or someone else's property even though no other vehicle is involved, do not fail to collect names and addresses and to note the conditions and layout where the incident occurred. And call the police if you or someone else is injured.

Even if your motor insurance will pay for part of the damage done, you may need compensation for your own injuries and for any claims on you for damages by other people whose property you have unavoidably destroyed or harmed. The person who caused the accident may be covered under the liability section of a household contents policy. He may not, however, be insured for such liabilities, and unless he is able and willing to pay up without more ado, you would have to issue proceedings on him through the courts. But before going to the trouble and expense of issuing proceedings, consider whether the other party would be able to pay up if you won.

pedestrians and cyclists

Where a pedestrian has caused an accident, remind him that if he has a household contents policy it is likely that its personal liability section covers him for a negligent act causing an injury or damage to another person. If his legal liability is not in doubt, you should ask him to pass your claim to his insurers so that you can get payment from him under that policy.

A pedal cyclist is not required by law to have insurance for third party claims. But he, too, may be covered by a household contents policy's liability section or may have taken out a separate cyclist's policy which will cover third party claims. You would have to show that the accident was due to the cyclist's negligence.

injured as a pedestrian or cyclist

When you are injured because a car has knocked you down – for example, while you were cycling, standing or walking at the side of the road or were on a pedestrian crossing, or a car drove through a red light and hit you – you can claim compensation from the driver. By law, he should be insured for injuries to a third party. If he was uninsured or did not stop and is not traceable, you may be able to claim on the Motor

Insurers' Bureau (New Garden House, 78 Hatton Garden, London EC1N 8JQ).

When the police arrive they will make notes and take statements from witnesses, even if you are in no state to do so.

Unless unconscious or in great pain, you should try to memorise what the driver of the car, or passers-by or helpers, said at the time and, as soon afterwards as you possibly can, make a note of relevant remarks and try and contact witnesses.

Even if you do not seem to be badly hurt at the time, you should get the driver's name and address and the car's registration number, in case later some injury manifests itself, for which you may want to claim compensation.

If, after an accident, your injuries are such that you think you do not require medical attention, it may nevertheless be sensible to visit your general practitioner and tell him what happened. Certain injuries may not be apparent immediately.

The burden of proof is on you as plaintiff that the defendant has been negligent; he may put forward a case for contributory negligence on your part. The police report, and any subsequent prosecution proceedings, will be important evidence for your claim against the driver.

You should be prepared to have to pursue your claim vigorously, and in most cases, your best interests will be served by getting legal advice from the outset.

cyclist

A cyclist who has been involved in a road accident can take advantage of a solicitors' directory for cyclist compensation, initiated by Friends of the Earth. A countrywide network is planned, providing leaflets at bike shops, libraries and other outlets, which advise cyclists to contact either their own solicitor or Friends of the Earth, 377 City Road, London EC1V 1NA. FoE will then forward the name of a solicitor with a form to be completed giving basic details of the accident. The solicitor will have agreed to give free legal advice on whether there are grounds for a claim for compensation and will take on the case, if requested.

ACCIDENT CAUSED BY ANIMAL OR CHILD

Under common law, everyone has a duty to take all reasonable steps to prevent injury being caused to another person. The 'duty of care' extends to ensuring that one's child or one's dog does not cause an accident – for example, by running into the road.

by animals

Statute law has codified the common law to some extent regarding animals. In general terms, animals must be kept under proper control. If a dog (but not, it seems, a cat) causes an accident on a road or anywhere else and the owner is traceable, he can be sued for the animal's behaviour if the escape of the dog and the subsequent accident can be held to be due to the owner's negligence.

If an accident is caused by livestock on a road or elsewhere, for any claim to succeed the injured person would have to show that the farmer had failed in his duty to do what is reasonably necessary to ensure that his livestock do not wander away.

The Animals Act 1971 includes a section which modifies the general duty of care:

> "Where damage is caused by animals straying from unfenced land to a highway, a person who placed them on the land is not to be regarded as having committed a breach of the duty to take care by reason only of placing them there if the land is common land, or is land situated in an area where fencing is not customary, or is a town or village green, and he had a right to place the animals on that land."

The law draws a distinction between 'dangerous' animals and animals which are naturally domesticated in this country, such as dogs, cats, cows and horses. Someone injured by an animal in the domesticated category will normally only be able to sue successfully if it can be proved that there was a failure to take reasonable care or exercise reasonable control of the animal – for example, a rider failing to control a horse while using the road.

If you are injured by an animal not commonly domesticated in this country, the keeper of the animal will be held liable without your having to prove negligence. Similarly, if you can prove that even a 'domesticated' animal was unusually prone to cause injury and that the owner or keeper specifically knew, or ought to have known of this, he will be liable without your having to prove negligence. (If the animal belongs to a child under the age of 16, the 'keeper' of the animal who is held responsible is the head of the household of which the child is a member.)

If the owner of a dog which attacks someone can show that at no time in the past had the dog exhibited any such tendencies, he would not be liable for the injury. Signs such as "beware of the dog" may be an indication that the owner is concerned that the dog is a creature of which the public should beware, and that you should take care. On the other hand, such a sign may be used as evidence that the owner should have been more careful.

in Scotland

The Animals Act 1971 does not apply to Scotland.

Whether an owner of animals is liable for accidents caused by their straying on roads depends on the circumstances. A farmer is liable if his cattle wander round town, but drivers should expect to find animals on unfenced country roads and should drive accordingly.

The owner of livestock is liable (under the Winter Herding Act 1686) for damage done by their straying on to other people's land and gardens. Liability exists even if he or she had taken reasonable steps to prevent straying.

When the new Animals (Scotland) Bill has been enacted (expected by April 1987), you will have to prove negligence even if you were injured by a vicious 'domesticated' animal. (This should be fairly easy if the keeper knew or ought to have known about the viciousness.) Where an animal belongs to a child under 16, the adult having actual care and control of the child is to be the 'keeper' and be jointly liable with the child for damage caused by the animal.

by children

The Consumer Publication *Children, parents and the law* explains that "there is no general basis on which parents are liable for the negligence of their children. A child's 'negligence' will be judged against the standard of care of a reasonable child of that age. Although someone under the age of 18 can be sued for damages, the practical disincentive is that he will not usually have any money. One obvious exception would be a child of 17 who has injured somebody while driving a car or riding a motor bike. In practice, because of compulsory insurance, such a case would not be different from one where a claim is brought against an adult. It is no defence for a motorist to say that he is a learner driver: he will be judged against the standard of the reasonably competent motorist.

"Under the age of 18 a person cannot be sued in his own name but must be represented by a guardian *ad litem*. Usually the court appoints a parent to be guardian *ad litem*, who conducts the action on the child's behalf and instructs a solicitor.

"A more difficult question is whether a parent can be personally liable for damage caused by a child due to the parent's negligent failure to supervise the child properly. There have been apparently similar cases decided differently where parents have given their child a gun without adequate instruction on how to use it or prohibition about where to fire it. Each case is considered on its facts. The relevant factors will be the age of the child, the dangerousness of the activity, any instructions or other protective steps taken by the parent, whether or not the parent knew the child was disobedient."

in Scotland

Girls below 12 and boys below 14 are sued in their own names and those of their parents. The parents control the case and instruct legal advisers on behalf of the child.

Older children who are still below 18 are also sued in their own names and those of their parents. But the parents merely agree to the child's decisions.

Where a child has no parents, or they refuse to act or have an adverse interest, the court appoints a *curator ad litem* to act on behalf of or to assist the child.

ACCIDENT INVOLVING PUBLIC AUTHORITIES

Most large public bodies, sections of national or local government or a company which is or used to be nationalised, such as the Post Office or British Telecom, are regulated and protected by one or more statutes. Therefore, if at any time you think you have a claim on a public body, the relevant legislation may lay down exactly what you – and they – can and cannot do. In some cases, public authorities have special defences not available to other organisations. But so far as any personal injury is concerned, no body can exclude or limit its liability for negligence. Signs such as "Persons travel at their own risk" do not protect the company if any personal injury arises from the negligence of that company or its servants or agents.

In the majority of cases, public authorities are just as accountable to an aggrieved party as is a private company or individual. For example, if a water main is being repaired and a hole has to be dug in the street, that hole must be protected properly and the water authority must take into account the fact that pedestrians may walk along a pavement carelessly and that some pedestrians may be blind. If proper barriers and warning lights and signs are not erected, the water authority could face a claim for damages from anybody who walked along the street and fell down the hole.

One difficulty encountered with public authorities is the question of whom to sue: in the above example, the local authority, whose responsibility it is to ensure that pavements are kept in good order? or the water authority who actually dug the hole? Your solicitor will have to decide what specific negligence or breach of statutory duty caused the damage or injury; your claim lies against the party who was responsible.

All public authorities have a duty to ensure that their particular sphere of responsibility is carried out in a proper fashion and will have to bear liability if it is not. In cases of large public bodies, the questions of reasonableness and foreseeableness also arise. A defect in a pavement does not necessarily mean the local authority are liable. They cannot be expected to know, for instance, that a lorry mounted the pavement and broke a paving stone only the day before you tripped over it. If they can show (and they generally keep a register for this purpose) that they have inspected the area at intervals appropriate to the degree of use of the particular area, and have had any defects repaired, a claim on them may not succeed.

pavements
The local highway authority has a duty to maintain pavements so as to be reasonably safe for pedestrians.

A National Consumer Council review of the pedestrian environment will be published in March 1987. It reports that some local authorities, when a claim is made for injuries caused by tripping over defective or uneven paving, propound that there is a legal ruling that an obstruction or unevenness of less than $\frac{3}{4}$ of an inch (20 mm), or even up to 1 inch, is not a hazard, and the local authorities – or their insurers – therefore disclaim responsibility. But the law (in the Highways Act 1980) lays down no precise measurement for what can be deemed a dangerous obstruction – the duty is to maintain "a state of repair in which a reasonable person would expect to find the highway". The lack of precision in the regulations about the duty to maintain highways and pavements can be to your advantage, and negotiations may lead to an acceptable *ex gratia* payment. But the NCC report warns that "to succeed at law in obtaining compensation for a pavement accident, a pedestrian must first prove that the pavement was dangerous to pedestrians; secondly, that there was a failure to repair that danger; thirdly, that as a result of failing to repair that danger, damage was caused to the pedestrian."

It will help your claim if it can be shown that someone else has previously reported or complained about the defect that caused your injury. The NCC found that many councils have failed to establish a formal system for complaints. A minority operate a 'postcard notification scheme', whereby reply-paid cards are distributed locally – either house to house or at doctors' surgeries, some post offices, libraries, community centres and suchlike – for any citizen to complete with details about inadequate maintenance or complaints about pavement-related problems.

Where the state of the road or pavement caused the accident, the local authority may suggest a meeting at the site (if they do not, you can ask for this to be arranged) within a day or two of the accident. At this meeting, do not expect to argue about who or what was at fault: it is basically to determine what did happen and where and how it happened. If these facts can be ascertained at this stage, pursuit of your claim should be more straightforward although the representative who turns up on a site inspection will not have the authority to agree anything. However, do be very careful what you say to any official. A careless remark could jeopardise your claim. It is best just to show them the area of the accident.

Alternatively or additionally, go back yourself and take a few photographs of the uneven slab, broken-down kerb, unguarded hole. Include a rule or other indication of its dimensions, so that they can see what you are talking about.

The **Pedestrians Association** (1–5 Wandsworth Road, London SW8 2XX) has a helpful leaflet *Falls on the footway* (single copy free – send stamped addressed envelope), giving advice on what you should do when claiming compensation and explaining what the highway authority will do. It includes a compensation claim form to be sent to the solicitor of the appropriate authority with brief details of where and how the fall occurred and a description of injuries and/or belongings damaged.

The Association also has pro forma cards (£1 for 10) on which a dangerous pavement surface can be reported to the local authority surveyor, with the warning to the council that "A copy of this card . . . will be used as evidence to support a claim for compensation should a pedestrian subsequently suffer personal injury before a repair has been effected."

The annual subscription for membership of the Pedestrians Association (incorporating the National Campaign for Safe Walking) is £4.

where to claim

It may not always be easy to ascertain which person in a large organisation should be approached. If unsure, try the public relations office or customer relations department. You could telephone the main office initially to ask about any claims procedure.

If the accident occurred on a train, write to the local area manager of the British Railways Board. If it happened on a London bus or underground, telephone LRT's Risk Management Services on 01-387 3400.

A country-wide service may use a number of different companies to operate in different areas so you need to contact the head office, asking either for the name and address of the relevant local company or for your claim to be passed on. For example, if the accident occurred on a National Express coach, write to the service standards manager, National Express, 1 Vicarage Road, Edgbaston, Birmingham B15 3ES, giving details of route, day, time, place when the accident occurred; the information will be passed to the relevant coach company for the area.

local authority

Which council is responsible for a particular service – the county, district or parish council – can be confusing, and for some there is no absolute rule. It is possible for one type of council to provide a service for which another is legally responsible. For example, a district council might take responsibility from a county council for maintaining certain types of road.

There are two kinds of local authority **in Scotland**: regional councils provide services such as roads and public transport, and district councils deal with housing, recreation etc. The Western Isles, Orkney and Shetland each have an islands council which runs all services.

The local telephone directories list local authority departments (roads, for instance, may be under the 'highways department' or the 'department of transportation'). Most local authorities have a general information or enquiry service with a telephone number.

If the accident happened in your own area, you will probably know the whereabouts of the main council offices (where you send your payment for rates) or you can find out locally (from library, citizens advice bureau, estate agent) where to write or call. But when you are not on home ground, you may have more difficulty in knowing whose local authority area you are in. If your companion or a bystander cannot tell you, ask the police, or the hospital staff if your injuries require their attention.

claiming

When making a claim against a public authority, the action that has to be taken (including gathering evidence and time limits) is the same as for a claim against an individual. The difficulty in making a claim against a large or public body is that you may be met with a general air of unaccountability, with no one apparently personally responsible for dealing with your complaint.

Notify the authority of the accident as soon as you possibly can after it happens (or get someone else to do so for you if you are incapacitated) so that the powers-that-be can start making enquiries straight away from their staff about their version of the incident, before recollection is overlaid by time or exchange of conflicting views with colleagues. It is best to make a complaint as soon as possible, but there is no point in ringing up half an hour after an accident has occurred and expect comment or action: it usually takes two or three days for a report to reach the relevant department.

If you telephone to report the accident, it is essential to take down the name and position (and preferably extension number) of the person to whom you speak about it. You may need that person to corroborate that you did report the accident. Make a note straight away of the gist of your conversation: after a telephone conversation of importance, it is advisable to write a letter immediately confirming what was said. Keep a copy. Whenever you write, always keep a copy of your letter, so that you (or your solicitor later) can know exactly what you did say or ask.

The first letter you or your solicitor write should give brief details of what happened, when and where, including the name of any official or employee of the authority who was there or whom you informed at the time – for instance, conductor, guard, ticket collector, driver, station supervisor – and the facts and circumstances why you consider the authority to be liable.

You would be well advised to get the help of a solicitor. Most public concerns are insured for such eventualities, so you will most likely end up corresponding and negotiating with an insurance company.

Your case will be allocated a reference number. This should be quoted whenever writing to or telephoning the authority's department and/or the insurance company.

You will need to provide information as precise as possible about the conditions, the exact location of the incident, the time, and will have to marshall all the facts that could possibly be relevant. Evidence of witnesses and medical or other experts' reports, or valuations and receipts, will also be needed for your solicitor to work on.

You may have to be patient while pieces of paper go to and fro between you, your solicitor, the local authority or other body, the insurance company, but do not let a disproportionate amount of time elapse without some action.

If liability is accepted, you will be offered a compensatory payment. Where liability is not admitted, sometimes an *ex gratia* payment is offered. You and your lawyer have to decide whether to accept this or risk taking the case further.

ACCIDENT ON SOMEONE ELSE'S PROPERTY

The occupier of premises owes his visitors a 'duty of care': that they will be reasonably safe on his property. 'Visitors' are not only specific guests but anyone who has an overt or implied right to be on the property.

Anybody who is pursuing a lawful aim has an implied right to enter a property. That means that the postman and the milkman are perfectly entitled to walk on anyone's land to carry out their job. If an occupier does not wish to have the person on his land any longer, he is entitled to terminate that implied right by requiring them to leave – and they become trespassers if they do not.

A 'visitor', too, has a duty to be reasonably careful. But the occupier should be prepared for children to be less careful than adults.

Where damage is caused to you, as visitor, by a danger of which the occupier had warned you, the warning does not necessarily absolve him from liability. For instance, a mere warning that a path is unsafe is not enough if that path is the only means of getting to the front door: an alternative route to the house would have to be proffered (to the back door, perhaps). But if you then use the front path, the legal maxim *volenti non fit injuria* applies: you have voluntarily accepted the risk and the occupier is not liable if you then get hurt.

If you come on to land without the occupier's implied permission (in exercise of a private right of way or a public right of access, for example, or as a trespasser), he is not liable for any loss of or damage to your property. As far as personal injury is concerned, however, an occupier owes a duty of care to anyone who is not his visitor if he is aware of a danger or has reasonable grounds to believe that it exists, and the risk is one against which he may reasonably be expected to offer the other some protection. A simple warning notice, so long as it is sufficiently clear and obvious, may remove liability from the occupier.

claiming on a householder

If you are injured on someone else's property, remember that household contents insurance policies cover a liability claim by a third party (you), including an accident arising from the negligent act of a member of the policyholder's household or family. So, you should not feel inhibited about making a claim on your host, even if a close friend or relative. But if you are a member of the same household, a claim by you will not be covered by the insurance.

Cover is provided under the contents section of a household policy for liability as occupier of the property. Even where accidents in or around a house resulting in damage or injury are caused by the structure of the building (for example, defective guttering, loose floorboards), it is the owner-occupier's contents insurance, not buildings insurance, that covers claims for the damage caused. Buildings insurance gives cover for an owner who is not the occupier – for example, a landlord.

Whoever you claim on has to comply with his insurers' notification conditions if he wants the protection of his policy. Accepting an apology and offer of payment from the house-holder may not be to your advantage: by doing this, he will be disobeying the terms of his insurance which are conditional upon his not admitting liability or paying out without his insurers' agreement. This means that if your injury worsens or any damage proves more extensive (and expensive) and you want to claim more than the payment he has made to you personally, his insurers could repudiate the insurance and refuse to take on the claim.

You should be quite formal about claiming, however well

you know the person. Write a short simple letter, setting out briefly the date, time, place and facts of the incident, stating that you hold the householder responsible and ask that your letter be sent on to his insurers. (You could send with it a friendly covering letter explaining that the enclosed letter is necessarily formal, for the insurers.)

You have no right to ask to be told the identity of the insurers and, if you happen to know who they are, no right to make direct contact with them unless and until they invite you to do so.

The insurers will deal with the claim direct with you (or your solicitor). Unless a dispute arises over the question of liability, the policyholder may not be required to give evidence and may even not be told the outcome of your claim by the insurers.

Your claim may be met by a denial of liability from the householder's insurers, perhaps on tactical grounds to improve the insurers' bargaining position or on legal grounds. At this stage, if not earlier, you should get expert advice. You will have to provide details of the injury or damage and support your claim by bills, receipts, valuations and descriptions of property damaged; for an injury claim, medical reports will have to be submitted, and an account of expenses incurred because of the injury and any anticipated future loss or expenses.

when shopping

Your rights in shopping are twofold: to be protected from structural hazards as a 'visitor' to the shop premises, and to be sold items which are safe to use as well as of merchantable quality and fit for their purpose.

When you are injured or your clothes or belongings damaged in a shop, you should at once bring it to the attention of the most senior member of staff you can get hold of. Also ask anyone in the shop who saw what happened at the time to be prepared to give their account of the incident, and take names and addresses. If the accident seemed due to a careless act by one of the shop assistants, be sure to note his or her name or number.

Unless you are already speaking to the owner, find out the name of the owner or whoever is responsible for the establishment (manager, director, partners, franchisee) and where you should write to him. You should send a brief account saying what happened and what you consider was the cause, that you hold the shop or the shop assistant responsible, and that you will be asking to be compensated for the injury or damage resulting from the negligence.

However apologetic and sympathetic the shopkeeper may be at the time, it is his legal liability that you have to prove – moral conscience and personal regrets are of little avail when it comes to claiming compensation at law.

The shop should be insured for liability for damage or injury sustained by anyone lawfully on the premises, such as a customer slipping on a wet floor or caught in a defective door, and the result of an employee's negligence – a customer tripping over a carelessly placed box, hit by an object dropped from a shelf.

Proving negligence may be difficult: the shop will do all it can to protect itself. Your solicitor may need to write a strongly worded letter (or two) or you may need a surveyor to report on structural defects. Be prepared to have to refute an allegation that your negligence contributed to the incident.

To avoid admitting liability, an *ex gratia* payment may be offered and you will have to decide whether it is acceptable or whether to pursue your claim further.

damaged by what you bought

Under the present law, a buyer who is injured by a defective product can sue the shop that sold him the product. In the right circumstances, the claim will succeed because there is a condition implied in any contract of sale that the product is reasonably fit for its purpose. But the right to sue under the contract is available only to the person who actually bought the article: if a member of his family or anyone else uses it and is injured by it, they have no rights against the shopkeeper because they had no contract with him. However, such a person will be able to sue the shop under the law of tort because shops owe a duty of care to all persons who may be affected by a defective product sold by them.

A claim made against the manufacturer will only succeed if it can be proved that the manufacturer had been negligent in not taking reasonable care in the production of the article – that is, in researching, designing, making and promoting the product. The burden of proof is on the claimant.

You will certainly need legal help with a claim for compensation after an injury or damage caused by a defective manufactured product, especially if you had not bought it yourself.

The Consumer Protection Bill, at present before Parliament, seeks to make it a criminal offence to supply unsafe goods. It also introduces the concept of strict liability for manufacturers or producers. This will mean that someone injured by a defective product will no longer have to prove negligence on the part of the manufacturer or producer, only that the product had a defect which caused the damage or loss.

ACCIDENT IN THE HOME

Accidental damage to property may be covered by a household contents insurance policy if you have been paying the higher-than-standard premium. This includes cover for careless actions, such as paint dropped on the carpet, smoke damage, scorching. A policy may exclude damage done by pets, or damage to clothing, or to brittle articles in the course of ordinary use.

But you cannot claim on your household insurance for an injury you yourself receive from an accident in your own home, unless an outsider was responsible.

You may be able to take legal action against the person who caused the accident – a builder, for instance, leaving an unsecured floorboad that causes you to trip and fall. You have to establish his or her liability in the same way as for any other accident claim.

avoiding accidents

You should try to make certain that, as far as is possible, your home is accident-proof. Stair rails, mats, rugs and other floor coverings should be secure, steps clearly marked and lit, electric wiring kept in good condition, heaters and open fires guarded, child-proof appliances used.

The **Child Accident Prevention Trust** has issued a pamphlet to help prevent accidents to children in the home, entitled *Keep Them Safe* (single copies available free from 75 Portland Place, London W1N 3AL). It gives details of traditional safety items, such as safety gates and fireguards, and describes newer products including glazing materials, coiled flexes for kitchen appliances and smoke alarms. It indicates the children's ages at which different items become important and includes information on cost, availability and relevant safety standards.

The crime prevention officer at the local police station can be asked to call to give free advice on how a home can be made more burglar-proof. No place can be made totally secure against burglars, but the more deterrents you have, the better your chance that the prospective burglar will decide it is a waste of time and go on to somewhere less difficult.

Where a burglar has damaged your house by breaking in or out, a household buildings insurance policy will cover the cost of the repairs or replacement needed.

compensation order

A criminal court has the power to make an order that a defendant who has pleaded guilty to a charge or has been convicted of a crime should pay compensation to the victim. Compensation orders will not be made if the offender is impecunious, or if the order will encourage him to offend, or if otherwise inappropriate.

Under normal circumstances, a compensation order is limited to the actual loss – for example, the cost of repairing a broken window. But, in some circumstances, the court can make an order for compensation for personal injury (including loss of wages). This does not preclude a claim on the criminal injuries compensation scheme – though any sum awarded by the criminal courts which was paid to you would be deducted.

criminal injuries compensation

There is a government-funded scheme to provide compensation for victims of 'crimes of violence' who would have little chance of obtaining redress from the perpetrator even if legal action could be brought successfully. The scheme is administered by the **Criminal Injuries Compensation Board**. A brief guide to the scheme plus a more detailed leaflet are available free from the CICB, Whittington House, 19 Alfred Place, London WC1E 7LG (telephone 01-636 9501).

Basically, you can apply for an *ex gratia* payment if you were injured

○ as a result of a crime of violence, or
○ when you were trying to stop someone from committing a crime, or
○ when you were trying to catch a suspect after a crime, or
○ when you were trying to help the police to apprehend somebody.

You can apply even if the person who committed the deed is not known or has not been brought to justice. You should, however, have reported the incident to the police without delay and tried to help them apprehend and convict the person. You can apply for compensation even if the injury was caused by someone who could not be held responsible under the criminal law – for example, a young child or a mentally ill person.

You have to apply within 3 years of the date you were injured. At present, there is a long delay in dealing with applications because of an accumulated backlog arising from an increasing number of claims.

Under the conditions of the scheme, the Board can pay out only if the injury is serious enough for the assessment of an appropriate award to come to more than a fixed amount (currently £550) and if you can convince the Board that you were not responsible in any way for the incident in which you were injured. The Board may also take into account your past character and way of life.

You have to complete a thorough 4-page application form; for someone under the age of 18, a parent or guardian also must sign the form. By signing the form, you authorise the Board to approach the police (your statements, any previous convictions), the doctors and others who treated you, your employers (your earnings, pension rights), government departments (payments received).

There is no fee to pay, and the work of investigating your claim is undertaken by the Board staff, who will write direct to the police and to your doctor and employer, as appropriate. You will be told what information and evidence you should provide – for instance, details of loss of earnings and out-of-pocket expenses incurred as a result of the injury.

the decision

A member of the Board (they are, at present, all lawyers) will make a decision whether, on the basis of documentary evidence, you can be paid compensation under the scheme and, if so, how much. A sum will be offered that is considered fair and reasonable under the circumstances.

Compensation is assessed by the Board in broadly the same way that courts of law assess damages. It includes payment to compensate for pain and suffering caused by the injuries, and may cover loss of earnings and out-of-pocket expenses. The assessed payment will be reduced to take account of social security payments you have received (deducted in full), an employer's pension, some kinds of insurance policies or other compensation already received for the injuries. The amount is likely to be much the same as the amount awarded by the courts in similar personal injury cases.

When you sign the form accepting an award, you have to agree to repay the Board out of any damages or compensation you may get later from any other source.

appeal

If you are not satisfied with this initial decision, you can ask for a hearing when three other members of the Board will consider your case afresh and in your presence. (Again, you may have to wait some time for this hearing to take place.)

Hearings are held in private and are as informal as possible. You have to arrange for any witnesses you want to call to be present. You may be able to claim reasonable expenses for yourself and your witnesses coming to the hearing.

You can bring a friend or legal adviser to help you. The Board does not pay legal costs and legal aid is not available. Even though costs cannot be recovered, in serious cases it may well be worthwhile consulting a solicitor, particularly on an appeal.

payment

The compensation is usually paid as a lump sum, by cheque. More than one payment may be made where an applicant's eligibility for compensation has been established but a final award cannot yet be calculated – for example, where only a provisional medical assessment can be given in the first instance. Unlike a common law damages claim, a CICB claim can be reopened in certain circumstances.

support for victim

There is an increasing concern about the emotional and psychological effect of a criminal assault on the victim.

Victims' support schemes are established in many parts of the country to offer personal support or practical help to anyone in getting over an attack.

The police often refer people for such help, but anyone can contact a local scheme direct without involving the police. You will be put in touch with someone with whom to talk through problems and reactions, including advice on difficulties that may have to be faced during a court case. The schemes provide only personal support: financial compensation is not included.

The **National Association of Victims Support Schemes** (17A Electric Lane, London SW9 8LA; telephone 01-326 1084) can tell you whether there is a support scheme in your area; so can the local police, or you may find a leaflet in your citizens advice bureau or library.

ACCIDENT AT WORK

Any employer has a duty to provide a reasonably safe place of work. In some cases, strict liability is imposed by statute, such as the requirement under the Factories Act that moving machinery be fenced. In circumstances where there is a strict liability, a defendant will be liable even if he has taken all reasonable precautions: failure to fence machinery is deemed to be a breach of the statutory duty owed by the employer to an employee which, if an injury results, gives rise to a cause of action in damages.

Normally, however, the employer is expected to ensure, as far as is reasonably practicable, that the factory or office or other place of work is safe to enter and walk about in: floors kept in good condition, with no uneven surfaces which might cause someone to trip, no slippery patches which might result in a fall and an injury. All equipment should be safe to use with proper guards fitted and instruction given in the use of any inherently dangerous equipment, proper supervision pro-vided and only trained employees allowed to use the equipment. If an employee disobeys safety instructions and is thereby injured, contributory negligence may apply.

health and safety standards
An employer has a duty to do everything reasonably possible to ensure that his premises are safe from accidents and, if an accident does occur, that it can be dealt with speedily and without further risk. Safety equipment has to be provided, including fire extinguishers and, where appropriate, protective clothing such as gloves, goggles and masks. There should be adequate first aid arrangements.

enforcement
The Health and Safety Commission is responsible for making arrangements for the enforcement of standards of safety as laid down by the Health and Safety at Work Act 1974 and related legislation. The Commission operates through the Health and Safety Executive and through local authorities' environmental health officers.

Health and Safety Executive (HSE) inspectors are responsible for enforcing health and safety legislation in industrial undertakings such as factories, mines, building sites and farms. Environmental health officers (EHOs) are responsible for commercial premises such as offices, shops and warehouses. There is no difference between HSE inspectors and environmental health officers in relation to their powers under the Act. The only difference is in the premises they inspect, as laid down in regulations.

Inspectors go to visit places of work to check that adequate safety standards are being maintained and to warn and advise on hazards. An employee (and an employer) who is concerned about the safety of his workplace can contact an environmental health officer at the local authority offices or call on an HSE inspector for help. A leaflet giving addresses and telephone numbers of the HSE area offices, showing the district each covers, is available from Broad Lane, Sheffield S3 7HQ (telephone 0742 752539) with other publications and information about HSE's activities.

reporting an accident

Employers (and the self-employed) have a statutory duty to ensure that certain injuries in specified circumstances are reported to the Health and Safety Executive. (This is to enable statistics to be kept, and investigations and preventive action taken where necessary,) The Reporting of Injuries, Diseases and Dangerous Occurrences Regulations 1985 (referred to as RIDDOR), which have been in force since 1 April 1986, require specified major injuries from accidents at work and those that necessitate the injured person being kept in hospital for more than 24 hours, to be reported immediately. If an injury causes incapacity for more than 3 days, the employer must report it in writing within 7 days of the accident, on a prescribed form, to the HSE area office or local authority's environmental health department, as appropriate.

The Health and Safety Executive's publications include a brief guide (for employers) to the requirements of RIDDOR and reporting an injury (HSE 11), available free from HSE area offices.

In addition, an employer is expected to keep a record of reportable injuries and dangerous occurrences, including date and time, place and circumstances of the accident and particulars of the injured person.

accident book

The employer has to keep an accident book as prescribed under the Social Security Act 1975 for premises on which 10 or more people are normally employed at the same time. This book should be kept in a place where it is readily accessible to all employees. Particulars of an accident can be entered in it by the injured employee or by someone on his behalf.

An entry in the accident book should be made as soon as possible after the event, and will count as formal notification to the employer. It is important that the entries are accurate and specific: not 'slipped on floor' but 'slipped on oil on floor'.

The employer should investigate every incident reported in the book. If he considers there is a discrepancy between the circumstances of the accident as recorded in the book and what he himself thought had happened, he will add his own version to the record.

Although reporting and/or recording the accident is in itself of no benefit to the injured employee, it does provide some evidence of what happened and can be relevant if a claim for damages is being made against the employer.

when an accident happens

The circumstances of an accident while at work may give rise to a claim for compensation.

Notice who was there at the time who might be able to make a statement or be called as an eye witness. Try to retain in your mind the position of objects or the condition of equipment or the state of flooring or lighting. You may be in pain or a state of shock at the immediate moment, but as soon as you have recovered a little, think back and reconstruct the event, preferably writing down the sequence of what it seems to you had happened.

Even if you do not seem to be incapacitated or disabled at the time, you should get from the social security office straight away form BI 95 on which you can apply for a declaration that the accident was an 'industrial' one. This will safeguard any future right to claim statutory benefit in case you later become incapable of work. It does not matter if you recover sufficiently afterwards not to need to follow up this declaration with a claim.

initiating a claim

If you claim damages because of an accident at work, your claim will almost certainly be dealt with by your employer's insurance company.

The Employers' Liability (Compulsory Insurance) Act 1969 requires employers (with the exception of local authorities, the police, nationalised industries) to have insurance to cover liability for bodily injury to an employee occurring in the course of his employment. This means that if you do have a claim against your employers because of the circumstances of the accident causing your injury, it should be met by their insurers. So, you do not need to feel hesitant or reluctant to claim – your employer will not have to pay out of his own pocket. The HSE short guide to the 1969 Act warns, however, that the Act "does not grant an employee an automatic right to compensation. The purpose of the Act is to ensure that, when an employee succeeds in a claim, his employer is insured and can pay the compensation that is due."

Even though you may believe the accident to have been the fault of a colleague at work, that should not put you off claiming.

If you belong to a trade union, you should discuss the circumstances of the accident and the possibility of a claim with your local union representative. Or have half-an-hour with a solicitor who is experienced in such claims and who operates the '£5 scheme' (many do not), or who participates in the free accident legal advice service (ALAS!).

Do not make a direct claim yourself without guidance and help. Your trade union representative may warn you of instances where direct claims have been 'bought off' very cheaply by insurers, where the individual should really have got more.

In the first place, a claim for compensation is sent to your employers personally. The employers will pass it on to their insurers, who may then send a claim form for you to complete.

You will have to explain briefly but clearly exactly what happened, what you were doing at the time, what other people around you were doing, the general conditions of light, temperature, cleanliness of the place.

evidence
You are likely to have witnesses of an accident at work, not only to that accident but to similar ones and dangers which have been relevant in the past. For example, if you are injured

by slipping on a floor, one of your colleagues may be able to say that he had fallen on that precise spot in the past or others may have done. This would help to substantiate your claim, particularly if they had complained to the employer or recorded the accident in the accident book. The accident book, in which all mishaps at work should be recorded, can be powerful evidence to your claim, if it shows that the particular type of accident had happened before and that the employer had failed to take the necessary action to do something about the danger.

It will have to be proved that it was your employer's negligence rather than your own carelessness or disobedience that caused the accident. Colleagues may be able to give evidence as to the training – or lack of training – which was provided for using a machine which caused the injury. In a unionised workplace, the safety representative should be particularly useful.

Your immediate injuries will have to be described, the treatment required, how the injury has developed and the disability it is causing now and the likely disability you will be left with and its effect on your future employment. You must expect to be asked for further medical particulars, including a doctor's or other practitioner's report, and perhaps a medical examination requested by the employer's insurers.

Your claim for general damages should include loss of earnings and future loss of earning capacity. If your claim is successful, the compensation you get will be assessed along the lines of the courts' awards for similar injuries. You may be offered an *ex gratia* payment. Your adviser (legal or union) will recommend whether you should accept this or not.

payments from the state under the industrial injuries scheme

Someone who is unable to work due to injuries caused by an accident at work does not have to satisfy the national insurance contribution conditions for statutory sick pay or sickness benefit. The payment is made automatically if you claim it, and if you are still unable to work after a 28-week period, you will go on to invalidity benefit.

The other main benefits under the industrial injuries scheme are

○ **disablement benefit** if you suffer a degree of disability above the set minimum (14%) for longer than 15 weeks, whether or not you are still unable to work
○ **reduced earnings allowance** if you suffer a degree of disability (assessed at not less than 1%) for longer than 15 weeks and your earnings are thereby reduced.

DHSS leaflet FB 15 is a guide to cash benefits if you are injured at work; leaflet NI 6 deals with industrial injuries disablement benefit.

general qualifying conditions

You must be an 'employed earner' and have suffered either personal injury caused by an industrial accident or a prescribed industrial disease.

employed earner

Everyone who is employed by someone else and is paid wages or a salary is an employed earner. That means anyone who pays class 1 national insurance contributions and also those who do not pay contributions only because their weekly earnings are below the statutory lower earnings level.

Generally, self-employed people who have complete control over their work do not count as employed earners. Many workers are only technically described as 'self-employed' for tax or other reasons. If you think that you might be treated as an 'employee', you should put in a claim.

industrial accident

The accident must have arisen out of your employment. There must be a connection between the accident and the injury, but the accident need not be the only cause – or even the main cause – and it need not be a direct cause.

Accidents may also be treated as arising out of employment if caused by another employee's misconduct or skylarking or negligence; also if the behaviour or presence of an animal (including a bird, fish or insect) caused the accident. Being struck by any object or hitting any part of your employer's premises, plant or machinery would qualify, so a fall at work is usually treated as an industrial accident.

The accident must have been in the course of your employment. You must have been at work, rather than travelling to or from work (unless travel is part of the work), and not breaking any rules. But breaking rules will not disqualify you if what you were doing was for the purpose of your employer's business and within the scope of your job. Misusing a machine will not disqualify you provided that you were using it for the purposes of your work.

industrial disablement benefit

Basic disablement benefit is a weekly payment for loss of physical or mental faculty as a result of an industrial accident. A claim cannot be made unless the disablement persists for more than 15 weeks after the accident or the onset of the injury. Thereafter, it will not be backdated farther than 3 months unless you can show good cause for a delay in claiming.

To claim after an industrial accident, complete form BI 100A, available from a social security office.

assessment of disablement
Entitlement to disablement benefit involves decisions on three points:

○ whether the relevant accident has resulted in loss of faculty
○ the degree of disablement resulting from the loss of faculty
○ what period is to be taken into account by the assessment.

loss of faculty
Whether there has been a loss of faculty depends on whether you are suffering from an impairment of the proper functioning of part of your body or mind. Disfigurement is treated as a loss of faculty.

degree of disablement
The assessment of the extent of disablement is always expressed as a percentage. Only if assessment is 14 per cent or more will you qualify for disablement benefit.

Regulations give some guidance as to the appropriate assessments: for example, loss of a hand to be assessed at 60 per cent and loss of one eye at 40 per cent. An assesment of 100 per cent does not denote total incapacity: for instance, loss of one hand and one foot would be assessed at 100 per cent, and so would absolute deafness.

The particular disablement is assessed by comparison with a person of the same age and sex whose physical and mental condition is unimpaired. Thus, if you are left-handed and lose your left hand, you should expect to receive a higher assessment than if a right-handed person had lost a left hand. Extraneous factors such as the distance of your home from the nearest public transport will, however, be ignored in assessing the percentage loss of, for example, an amputated foot.

The degrees of disablement for specified industrial injuries, as laid down by regulations, are listed in an appendix to the Child Poverty Action Group's *Rights guide to non-means-tested social security benefits* (1987 edition £4.50 from CPAG, 1–2 Bath Street, London EC1V 9QA).

other disablement

If you were disabled before the accident, your total disablement now should be assessed and from it deducted any disablement from which you would have suffered anyway had the accident not happened. This assessment is of the extent of disablement, not of loss of faculty. Where X-rays in a back injury case show a spinal abnormality which apparently predates the accident but had not previously produced any disablement noticeable to the claimant, no deduction would be made from the assessment of the present disablement. Where, however, the pre-existing loss of faculty would have caused disablement (for example, through arthritis) even if the accident had not taken place, a deduction will be made.

If you were injured in an industrial accident and then were disabled further from another cause, the effect of this later disablement is ignored in the assessment of your industrial injury if the degree of disablement solely due to the industrial accident was less than 11 per cent. If more, there will be added to that percentage the assessment of disablement resulting from the subsequent cause which you would not have suffered but for the industrial accident.

Where a claimant has a further industrial accident, the degrees of disablement resulting from both accidents will be aggregated. For the purpose of aggregation, the extent of disablement resulting from the first accident will be reassessed as at the date of the second accident.

If the assessment of the two injuries comes together to 14 per cent or more, you will qualify for disablement benefit.

what period

Where the assessment of disablement is 14 per cent or more, it will be either for a fixed period or for life, and the benefit awarded will be provisional or final.

A provisional payment is always for a fixed period and will be made where there is uncertainty about the prognosis. A new assessment will be made automatically at the end of the period. If you have a final assessment with payment for a fixed period and you are still disabled at the end of the fixed period, it is up to you to seek a new assessment by way of a review.

Where an assessment is of less than 14 per cent disablement, the period taken into account will be the period throughout which the claimant is likely to remain at least 1 per cent disabled.

the decision

Your case will be considered by the adjudicating medical authorities: either a single doctor or a medical board consisting of two or more doctors. Their function is to examine you medically and to decide on the degree of your disablement, and no more.

When you come before the doctor or medical board, you can have someone with you at the examination if this would help you. Make sure that you have a full list of your symptoms and current treatment to tell the doctor(s). Be exact and do not make yourself seem better able to manage than you really can.

The decision on your degree of disablement will be sent to you in writing.

If you are dissatisfied with the decision of the adjudicating medical authorities, there is a procedure for an appeal to a medical appeal tribunal. A member of a trade union should be able to get advice and help from the union representative when dealing with a benefit claim.

If your condition deteriorates during the period of assessment, you can seek a review at any time.

the amount of benefit

How much you will get depends on the extent of your disablement.

Where disablement is assessed as less than 14 per cent, no disablement benefit is paid. Where disablement is assessed as 14 per cent to 19 per cent, disablement benefit is paid at the 20 per cent rate. For disability assessed at 20 per cent or more, the percentage is rounded up or down to the nearest 10 per cent to allocate which rate of benefit is to be paid. For example, if your disablement is assessed at 34 per cent, you will get the 30 per cent rate of payment; if assessed at 35 per cent, you will get the 40 per cent rate.

From April 1987, the rates of disablement benefit are:

assessed percentage of disablement %	weekly payment %
100	64.50
90	58.05
80	51.60
70	45.15
60	38.70
50	32.25
40	25.80
30	19.35
20	12.90

The rates for a person under the age of 18 with no dependants are lower.

Disablement benefit is paid on top of any other national insurance benefits, such as statutory sick pay, sickness benefit, invalidity benefit.

If you are injured from a previous or a subsequent industrial accident, your total disablement benefit cannot amount to more than the 100 per cent rate.

constant attendance allowance

An allowance is payable to someone receiving disablement benefit at the 100 per cent rate who requires daily attendance as a result of the relevant loss of faculty, and is likely to go on needing it for a long time. The amount depends on the extent of attendance needed – part-time, normal, intermediate, exceptional.

Your entitlement to constant attendance allowance will be considered automatically at the time your disablement is assessed if the assessment is 100 per cent. If you find at a later date that you need the help of an attendant, a claim for constant attendance allowance should be made on form BI 104, available from social security offices.

reduced earnings allowance

An allowance is payable at the end of a 15-week qualifying period if, as a result of a loss of faculty assessed as at least 1 per cent, you are incapable, and likely to remain permanently incapable, of following your regular occupation and are incapable of following employment of an equivalent standard which is suitable in your case.

Your regular occupation is usually the occupation you had at the time of your accident (unless this was a job you were doing in a temporary capacity at the time).

Employment counts as 'equivalent standard' if the earnings are the same as in your regular occupation, including any opportunity to earn by working overtime.

The amount of the allowance is the amount by which earnings in an employment which is now suitable are less than current earnings in your regular occupation. The maximum allowance is £25.80 a week (from April 1987).

The reduced earnings allowance is an additional payment and it is payable to someone whose assessed disability is under 14 per cent and therefore does not entitle him to disability benefit. To anyone in receipt of disablement benefit, it is payable in addition.

REHABILITATION AFTER AN ACCIDENT

Injuries resulting from accidents range from apparently trivial hand injuries to major disasters such as a fractured spine. Even comparatively minor disability can be overcome more quickly with good rehabilitation and anyone with a severe disability should not be left to struggle alone or become resigned to incapacity.

The process of rehabilitation should start as early as possible: one school of thought says rehabilitation starts in the ambulance. Some people have found it difficult to make the fullest use of their impaired capacities when they have spent too long unable to do things after their accident and have become accustomed to this situation.

The effects of an injury are defined in various terms:

impairment: the damage or loss resulting from the injury

disability: the limitation of function caused by physical, mental or sensory impairment; the restriction or lack of ability in normal activities resulting from the impairment

handicap: the consequent economic or social disadvantage; the loss or limitation of opportunities to take part in the normal life of a community on an equal level with others, due to physical or social barriers.

The main effect is on the relationship between the individual and his or her environment.

Some people are minimally handicapped by severe disability while others are hugely handicapped by slight disability. This may reflect their job: a typist will be very handicapped by losing two fingers in an accident, an accountant may not be handicapped at all by such a loss. It may also reflect coping behaviour: someone with a previous tendency to worry or to be easily frustrated by difficulties will be less likely to overcome the problems of disability. Under stress, personality traits are exaggerated.

in the hospital

It may have been difficult in the anxiety of the moment to know what was happening, what has been done, and to find out what the prognosis is. Often, in the early days following an injury, people ask for information and are given it but their emotional state can interfere with their understanding and remembering what has been said. But when you are over the worst, do not be afraid to ask or ask again.

Doctors and surgeons may not feel able to commit themselves at an early stage about a serious injury. The doctor will give a 'best guess' answer, trying to be helpful because you have asked.

But not all complications are reasonably foreseeable and no two injuries are identical. Also, some doctors tend to think clinically rather than consider what effect the accident will have on the patient's way of life. A patient may be told that a fractured leg should unite in 8 to 12 weeks. He may therefore tell his employer that he will be back at work in 3 months, and his football club the same. Healing, which is the doctors' main concern, is one thing. Getting back to a normal active life which includes playing football may take very much longer. Moreover, the particular patient's fracture may take 16 weeks to unite.

rehabilitation and treatment

There are different schools of treatment, and often doctors with different approaches have patients in the same ward. So, people with similar injuries see the others following a different programme, which can confuse patients and relatives, unless they understand that there are different approaches to treating what appears to be the same condition.

While recovering, you should get treatment and assessment from the rehabilitation team, not just from the doctors who repaired the damage.

Rehabilitation after an accident consists of treatment to minimise functional loss (largely the concern of doctors and therapists) and the management of a permanent disability – a coordinating function of the occupational therapist, the social services, the family, and the individual himself.

Many people can do much to rehabilitate themselves if they are given proper advice and instruction – for instance, about exercises to build up muscle strength and mobilise stiff joints after a fracture. Good rehabilitation may also help to avoid later problems, such as osteo-arthritis. Being given precise short-term goals, such as managing to put on socks and shoes or walking a measured distance, will help. Such self-help works best for someone who is well-motivated.

Someone who has a hand injury or limitation of movement in a joint such as the elbow, will only regain good function if it is exercised intensively soon after injury. These joints stiffen very quickly if not moved and may then never move fully again. (In a case in Scotland in 1980, the judge reduced the damages awarded because the claimant had not followed his surgeon's advice to exercise his hand.)

physiotherapy
The extent of soft tissue damage caused by the accident having been assessed, the physiotherapist will devise means to enable you to regain functional ability by relieving pain and reducing any swelling which may impede movement. The physiotherapist will help you to mobilise joints and to strengthen muscles affected by the accident and assist you to regain confidence and make your own maximum efforts towards

recovery. You can be taught by the physiotherapist how to use crutches and how to manage stairs.

It is important to get clear instructions: for example, if your leg has been put in plaster, can you take a bath or shower? If you have been given crutches, when can you take weight on your leg? How soon should you exercise the damaged part and how hard should you work at this? Ask for written instructions, if necessary.

occupational therapy

The occupational therapist assesses what patients are capable of doing, what they need to do and how they are likely to manage at home or at work, and arranges for the necessary aids and adaptations to help with routine tasks of daily life.

Occupational therapy also provides activities designed to speed up recovery and maximise function. Graded activities are used to mobilise joints, improve coordination, concentration, memory span and to help re-orientation. Occupational therapists make sure that when patients are ready to go home they will be able to cope.

medical rehabilitation centres

Rehabilitation after a severe injury can take a long time. An important aspect of rehabilitation is assessment and reassessment of capacity, so that the individual and the family can know what to expect, and plans can be made for the future. If this is not being provided by the hospital, specialist services may be required.

Medical rehabilitation centres (or demonstration centres as they are also called) provide more intensive rehabilitation than is usually available in a general hospital. Patients may attend all day, five days a week, for intensive physiotherapy, including gymnastics, and for occupational therapy. There are about 30 NHS medical rehabilitation centres around the country, mostly residential or partly so. A list of demonstration centres is available from the DHSS Health Services Division, Alexander

Fleming House, Elephant and Castle, London SE1 6BY. Some units, such as Mary Marlborough Lodge at the Nuffield Orthopaedic Centre in Oxford, specialise in treating severely disabled people.

after a head injury

Effects which follow many head injuries, even those regarded as minor, include poor memory, poor concentration, learning and information-handling difficulties, reduced stamina, irritability, anxiety/depression and altered patterns of sexual activity. All of these can interfere with a person's rehabilitation and eventual re-entry into a normal way of life.

Many resulting problems are not immediately apparent. Apart from the more obvious effects, such as paralysis of parts of the body or defective vision, personality changes and less stable patterns of behaviour are not uncommon – a previously placid person may become difficult and irritable. Sometimes the result is not so much a change of personality as an exaggeration of former traits which were acceptable in their previous form but now constitute anti-social behaviour. Previous personality is a critical factor in the eventual outcome.

A psychologist can assess the problems resulting from brain damage following head injury, advise on ways of managing behavioural problems, devise treatment programmes and monitor progress.

The most marked recovery normally occurs within the first six months but improvement can be expected over the next three to five years. There may be long periods when the person has reached a plateau but this does not mean that further improvement may not still occur.

back at home

An occupational therapist should visit the home before a patient is discharged if there is likely to be a problem there. Sometimes, patients are allowed home on crutches without realising that they will not be able to carry even a cup of tea from one room to another. Or someone who can just about manage to climb five stairs in the hospital goes home to a flat on the third floor with no lift and it takes two hours to reach the flat's front door.

The hospital social worker liaises between hospital and the community, arranging for any services that may be required at home.

Some services in the community are the responsibility of the national health service, others of the local authority, and others are provided by voluntary organisations locally or nationwide. The local branch of the Red Cross may be able to help with equipment through its medical loan service, and has nursing and welfare officers who visit.

To find out what services exist in your area other than through the local authority social services department, ask at the citizens advice bureau or local council of voluntary organisations. Some of these services are supported by the local authority, others by voluntary groups and local churches.

Who does what and what is available varies from place to place.

The general practitioner is the link person who is responsible for authorising any NHS help that a patient may need at home such as a district nursing sister to change dressings, give injections, perhaps give a blanket bath; a bathing attendant to give baths at home (a male attendant is sometimes available).

Community or domiciliary physiotherapists (usually based at the local district general hospital but sometimes attached to a general practice) give treatment at home; this may include various electrical treatments, teaching suitable home exercise or advising on walking aids and monitoring progress.

A social worker can be contacted through the local authority social services department for help with personal, family and practical matters and may arrange for domestic help where this is required.

For a home help to come and do some housework, shopping, cooking, contact the home help organiser of the local authority. There may be a charge, depending on the local authority and your means.

Meals-on-wheels, usually lunch on (some) weekdays, can be delivered to the home for someone who has difficulty preparing meals. This can be arranged through the social services department, and a charge will be made according to the local authority's policy.

In some local authority areas, there are community occupational therapists who can come to advise on aids and adaptations such as bath rails, raised lavatory seats, handrails, ramps, and arrange for their provision through the social services department.

driving and not driving

After an accident, your injuries may make it unsafe or illegal for you to drive. Talk to the doctor treating you about the implications of your condition and driving – and do not drive until you are sure you can safely do so medically and legally.

All drivers are required by law to inform the Driver and Vehicle Licensing Centre (DVLC) in Swansea when they become aware of any disability expected to last for more than three months which is, or may become, likely to affect fitness as a driver. This requirement is printed on all driving licences.

You should write a letter to the DVLC (Swansea SA99 1TU) explaining what has happened to you. You will be sent a medical questionnaire and will be asked to give your permission for the DVLC medical branch to approach your GP or other doctor for further information. You may also be required to attend a medical examination. On completion of the enquiries, a decision will be made about your driving licence. It may be revoked outright, or revoked with immediate re-issue of a short-period licence (up to 3 years), or limited to driving a suitable adapted vehicle. There is a right of appeal against the revocation or restriction of a licence.

If someone who has not informed the authorities of a relevant disability is involved in a motor accident, he may find that he is not covered by his insurance because his driving licence is no longer valid.

Even if the disability is not expected to last three months, someone who is driving a car while handicapped – for example, in a plaster cast that limits the ability to control the car – may find this affects his insurance cover. It is the policy-holder's duty to disclose to his insurers any change in his circumstances relevant to his driving. If asked, the insurance company will usually agree to continue the cover for driving if there is minor disablement, especially if it is temporary.

help when severely disabled

Anyone who has suddenly become severely disabled after an accident will not only have the obvious physical problems inherent in being confined to a wheelchair or losing a limb or having a disfigured face, but may also have psychological problems.

Becoming disabled is a shock. There will be a sense of loss, a feeling of grief and of emotional vulnerability. It may be difficult to have to accept a degree of dependence on others.

Disability inevitably affects relationships with other people, and can be a burden for the family and for the disabled person. Both sides may need counselling to help work through their difficulties, to put their problems in perspective so that they can see for themselves the relevant options, to make choices and take appropriate action. Sometimes 'peer counselling' is useful: someone with a spinal injury can help a newly injured spinal patient by listening and providing information.

The **Spinal Injuries Association** (76 St James's Lane, London N10 3DF, telephone 01-444 2121) is a self-help group for people with spinal cord injuries and their families, run by the spinally injured themselves. There is a personal injury claims service and an information service for individual queries, a welfare service to sort out problems, a care attendant agency for emergency short-term help and other services. Members get a quarterly newsletter with information on current activities, and there are publications about different aspects of coping with spinal injury.

Severe brain damage caused by a head injury increases the prospective risk of epilepsy.

The **British Epilepsy Association** (Anstey House, 40 Hanover Square, Leeds LS3 1BE, telephone 0532 439393, with 5 regional offices) provides support for those with epilepsy, through groups and by pamphlets and statements on various aspects of the problem and how others can help, including employers. The **National Society for Epilepsy** runs the Chalfont Centre for Epilepsy (Chalfont St Peter, Gerrards Cross,

Bucks SL9 0RJ, telephone 02407 3991) which provides assessment, treatment and residential care, including a sheltered workshop. Both organisations provide a small identifying card to be carried by anyone likely to have an epileptic attack so that people around can know what is happening and what to do (and not to do).

Headway (National Head Injuries Association, 200 Mansfield Road, Nottingham NG1 3HX, telephone 0602 622382) is an organisation of self-help groups throughout the country, providing support and counselling to victims, and to families or carers faced with the sudden trauma of having to cope with someone who has had a serious head injury or is brain-damaged. Social and other activities and advice are available to help rehabilitate the damaged person and to help the carers share their experiences.

Families may need counselling to help cope with a changed personality and strange unacceptable behaviour, particularly where they also have to face up to diminished expectations.

care at home

There are various organisations which aim to relieve the strain on the carers of disabled people from time to time. This help does not replace statutory services but aims to supplement them.

Crossroads Care Attendant Schemes have been set up in many parts of the country to provide individual help for disabled people living at home either on their own or with family or friends, who are in need of reliable trained care at crucial moments. Further information and a leaflet listing all the places where a Crossroads scheme exists is available from the Association of Crossroads Care Attendant Schemes Ltd, 94 Coton Road, Rugby, Warwicks CV21 4LN (telephone 0788 73653).

The Leonard Cheshire Foundation (26–29 Maunsel Street, London SW1P 2QN, telephone 01-828 1822) runs 23 family support services throughout England, offering part-time care for disabled people who live in their own home or with their family. The Foundation's handbook *Family Support Services for physically and mentally handicapped people in their own homes* (£1.50) gives details of how to set up a family support service.

The Association of Carers (1st floor, 21–23 New Road, Chatham, Kent ME4 4QJ, telephone 0634 813981) offers support and information to anyone looking after a disabled person at home. Membership brings access to advice on sources of financial help, on adaptations and equipment, on statutory services, as well as personal support and reassurance and a chance to meet and help other carers. *Help at hand* is a signpost guide (free to members) covering the emotional aspect of caring as well as state benefits and services.

Community Service Volunteers (CSV) runs the Independent Living Scheme (ILS) which matches young volunteers with individuals needing a high level of care so that they can live in their own home instead of an institution. The volunteers are untrained and work to the direction of the disabled person. There is a charge; local authorities will often sponsor people and bear this cost themselves. For further details, contact the national headquarters: Community Service Volunteers, 237 Pentonville Road, London N1 9NJ (telephone 01-278 6601).

sources of information
There are many organisations specifically to help disabled people and encourage them to participate in normal activities. Some are run by disabled people themselves; some are members of the **British Council of Organisations of Disabled People** (St Mary's Church, Greenlaw Street, London SE18 5AR, telephone 01-854 7289).

DIAL is a free, confidential service of information and advice for disabled people, their families and professionals. There are over 75 DIAL groups, manned by people with a direct experience of disability. Each group is organised independently and has developed its own service. The national association is DIAL UK, Dial House, 117 High Street, Clay Cross, Chesterfield, Derbyshire S45 9DZ; telephone 0246 864498.

The **Disabled Living Foundation** (380–384 Harrow Road, London W9 2HU, telephone 01-289 6111) runs an information service on all aspects of disability, and a centre where aids and equipment can be seen and tried by appointment. (The DLF can supply the addresses of similar centres in different parts of the country.) The DLF has published *Coping with disability* (£8 including postage) which gives detailed advice on the subject.

There are a number of other books giving information and advice to disabled people. For example:

The *Disability Rights Handbook* is published annually by the Disability Alliance Educational and Research Association (25 Denmark Street, London WC2H 8NJ; 1987 edition £2.80, quarterly updating supplements £1.60 each). It has a long list of general and specialist organisations dealing in some way with disability, including specific disability groups and self-help groups. Relevant local government departments and local self-help advice centres are also listed.

The *Directory for disabled people – a handbook of information and opportunities for disabled and handicapped people* is available (£13.50 including postage) from the Royal Association for Disability and Rehabilitation (RADAR, 25 Mortimer Street, London W1N 8AB, telephone 01-637 5400). RADAR can also provide general information, especially on employment, education, access, housing and holidays.

The Disablement Income Group (Attlee House, 28 Commercial Street, London E1 6LR, telephone 01-790 2424) campaigns to improve the financial position of disabled people. It runs an advisory service and has a network of branches. Its publications include *Compass*, a regularly updated direction finder for disabled people (£2.60 including postage), *The chance to work* (£3.35 including postage), and leaflets about social security benefits.

allowances from the state

Anyone who needs intensive care at home for a prolonged period should check entitlement to attendance allowance. This is a statutory non-means-tested payment, tax free, payable weekly to anyone whose physical or mental disability necessitates being cared for by someone else during the day and/or through the night. DHSS leaflet NI 196 gives current rates, and leaflet NI 205 explains the conditions and incorporates a claim form. After you have completed the claim form, a doctor will have to examine and report on you. It will be another 2 to 3 months before you get formal notification of the decision, and whether you will get the higher or the lower rate of allowance.

In addition, the person who is caring for you may qualify for invalid care allowance. This is a taxable weekly payment for anyone who spends a minimum of 35 hours a week looking after a disabled person, provided that the disabled person qualifies for attendance allowance (or constant attendance allowance due to an industrial injury). The conditions and a claim form for invalid care allowance are in DHSS leaflet NI 212.

DHSS leaflet HB 1 is a brief guide to the range of benefits and services which could help anyone who is handicapped and the family who is doing the caring.

mobility

When getting about is a long-term problem, a mobility allowance from the DHSS may be payable. This is paid weekly to someone unable or virtually unable to walk because of severe physical disability and likely to remain so for at least a year. It cannot be claimed after the age of 65. DHSS leaflet NI 211 gives details and includes a claim form.

The allowance could be used on taxis, or to pay for the petrol when a friend drives you, or to pay for a car or powered wheelchair through the Motability scheme. **Motability** is an independent organisation, set up originally by government initiative, to help people who qualify for mobility allowance to hire or hire-purchase a car. Information leaflets and an application form are available from Boundary House, 91–93 Charterhouse Street, London EC1M 6BT (telephone 01-253 1211).

A person in receipt of mobility allowance need not pay for a vehicle excise licence and can obtain a disabled exemption certificate for the road tax disc.

A summary of state and local authority help with getting around is given in DHSS leaflet HB 4, including exemption from road tax on a car you own but are too disabled to drive.

Motoring and mobility for disabled people (£4, published by RADAR, 25 Mortimer Street, London W1N 8AB) includes details of special purpose vehicles, control conversions and adaptations. It includes a section on wheelchairs with information on choosing and using.

There are mobility centres where you can go for assessment of your driving abilities and needs. For example, the Department of Transport has set up MAVIS (Mobility Advice and Vehicle Information Service) at the Transport and Road Research Laboratory at Crowthorne, Berkshire (telephone 0344 779014). A range of adapted vehicles can be seen there and test drives undertaken. There are fees for assessment and advice on driving ability and car adaptation; general information on outdoor mobility and transport is free.

There are various assessment centres around the country, a few offering free facilities and others charging varying amounts for assessment. All offer free advice and some are able to offer help in choosing 4 mph pavement vehicles and help for disabled passengers as well as drivers. A Forum of Disabled Drivers' Assessment Centres has been formed: for information, contact the Banstead Place Mobility Centre, Park Road, Banstead, Surrey SM7 3EE; telephone Burgh Heath (07373) 51674.

The **Disabled Drivers' Association**, Ashwellthorpe Hall, Norwich NR16 1EX (telephone 050 841 449), is a self-help organisation which specialises in the mobility difficulties of drivers and passengers. There are local groups throughout the country where people with similar experience of disability are ready to give encouragement and help. Voluntary officers can help with individual problems; advice can be obtained about the choice of vehicle, conversions, insurance, benefits, holidays, services and access for disabled people.

concessions
There are concessions on rail fares for people with specified disabilities. Ask at a station or post office for the leaflet *British Rail and disabled travellers* and about the disabled persons railcard.

Under the Transport Act 1985, local authorities have discretionary power to grant concessionary bus fares to people with a handicap which seriously impairs their ability to walk and to those unable to drive or refused a driving licence on medical grounds.

the 'orange badge'
If your disability becomes permanent and causes you considerable difficulty in walking, you can apply to the local authority for an orange badge to display on a car which you are using as driver or passenger. This will allow the car to be parked free at meters for any length of time, and on single or double yellow lines in England and Wales for up to two hours with a special orange timing disc, without limit in Scotland. The national scheme does not apply in some inner London boroughs, where similar schemes operate for residents only.

If you think you may be eligible for an orange badge, you should apply to your local authority social services department; in Scotland, to the chief executive of your local Regional or Island council. Someone who gets a mobility allowance or a car supplied by a government department or a grant towards a vehicle is automatically eligible; in other cases, your doctor may be asked for confirmation of the severity of your disablement and need. There is no appeal if the social services department decides you are not eligible.

A Department of Transport leaflet about the orange badge scheme, and its conditions and use, is available from social services departments, CABx and other advice and information points.

WHEN YOU ARE GETTING BETTER

Getting on with rehabilitation and recovery will enable someone intending to return to work to do so as early as possible.

Claims for compensation for personal injuries are not usually settled until there is agreement that the claimant has recovered or as fully so as can be expected. Many people do go back to work before their claim is settled, but some could have returned even earlier.

It can be tempting, maybe at a subconscious level, to delay recovering fully and not to return to work because that implies recovery, until the case for compensation has been settled.

Ask your solicitor for specific advice as to when you should try to return to work. Legal opinion is roughly equally divided between the view that a better settlement will result if (a) you get back to work quickly, or at least show that you are trying hard, and (b) you do not go back to work and appear to be unemployable.

An injured person's lawyer, or perhaps trade union representative, will want the claim to maximise the effects of the accident. Your objective after an accident should be maximum recovery. Rehabilitation and the return to as normal a life as possible is more rewarding in the long run than squeezing more money out of the other side.

Six months after an accident is a critical time for someone who is off work, because the criteria for entitlement to state benefits change then. And some employers' sick pay schemes cease payment when someone has been away from work for so many months.

A longer than necessary period off work has other disadvantages. Delaying return to work can diminish the quality of life in social and psychological terms. Looking back to the past and recrimination about the accident is damaging; most people recover their self-esteem when they are back in the world of work and can look forward to the future.

GETTING BACK TO WORK

Most people who have become disabled as the result of an accident will want to keep their job or to find alternative employment, depending on the extent of their disablement.

When considering employment, it is the handicap that is more important than the disability. Someone could be disabled in strictly medical terms but have no handicap: for example, a facial disfigurement with no functional loss.

No matter how severe a disability is, it may have no impact on the job the person is employed to do. For example, a computer operator may, as a result of an accident, become deaf but because the use of hearing is not essential to his job, he may not need to change it.

Any newly disabled person should not become too pessimistic. A positive approach may help you to preserve your current job or to find another more easily. The first thing to do is to assess accurately the abilities you still have, despite the injury. Employers are interested in what you can do, not what you cannot do.

how much can you do?
A doctor is likely to be able to give an accurate assessment of your physical condition. His opinion about what you now cannot do, jobwise, is a factor in the assessment of damages you can claim if it affects your present and future earning capacity.

When the doctor says you are fit for work, but says that you can do "only light work", it is important that you discuss with the doctor precisely what he means by this, in relation to the nature of your own job. Ask him to specify any tasks that should be avoided. Doctors are not always aware of the real nature of patients' work, and therefore what they can or cannot manage to do in the context of the particular work circumstances. You should establish the exact nature of any medical restrictions especially if these are couched in general terms – for example, "no lifting" or "no standing". Clearly, more job opportunities are open to someone who can lift weights of, say, up to 14 lbs rather than no weights at all, or who can stand for an hour or so rather than being limited to purely sedentary work.

Trial spells back at work, reduced hours per day or days per week and flexible hours, are all possibilities.

resettlement advice

Advice can be sought from the disablement resettlement officer (DRO) at your local jobcentre. DROs are trained to help overcome the problems of disability associated with employment. There is a DRO attached to every jobcentre (look under 'Manpower Services Commission' in the telephone directory) and you can telephone or go in to ask for an appointment with him.

The DRO can help in a variety of ways. He can arrange meetings with your employer to discuss a change of employment within your residual capabilities, with or without aids or other adaptations. A person confined to a wheelchair would be handicapped by a building which could only be entered by the use of steps. If a ramp were built, however, there would be no handicap because the person could enter the building without assistance by means of the ramp.

The DRO can advise on alternative employment and put you forward for suitable vacancies. Where necessary, he can refer you to a training course or for occupational assessment at an employment rehabilitation centre.

advice for employers

Some employers may not understand the nature and effect of disability. For example, a person may, as a result of a head injury, suffer from epilepsy. The main difficulty which people with epilepsy face is the prejudices of others. A comparatively small number of people with epilepsy suffer from 'grand mal' seizures which would cause them to collapse, and even those who are prone to such seizures can have their frequency and intensity controlled by medication. In such cases, the greater handicap jobwise is generally the attitude of other people.

People who are newly disabled are likely to be unprepared for the negative reaction to their disability they may come up against in the employment field.

The Manpower Services Commission has drawn up a code of good practice on the employment of disabled people. The MSC issues pamphlets for employers about schemes for disabled workers, including ones on employing people with specific conditions, such as epilepsy or deafness. It runs a Disablement Advisory Service (DAS) to provide employers with practical advice and guidance on how to make full use of the services and abilities of disabled employees and how to fulfil their legal obligations towards disabled people. The various sources of help available through DAS include provision of various technical aids to employment and grants to help meet the cost of adapting premises or equipment.

Part of the duty of DAS disablement advisers is to become involved, on request, with newly disabled people who are in employment.

The Royal Association for Disability and Rehabilitation (25 Mortimer Street, London W1N 8AB, telephone 01-637 5400) is active in promoting the employment of disabled people and has published an *Employer's guide to disabilities* (£19 including postage). RADAR can answer general queries and offer advice on how to obtain employment. RADAR's publications include *Into work*, a loose-leaf pack for disabled people (free but send a 10in. × 7in. stamped addressed envelope).

employment options

There are a number of options, depending partly on the extent of your functional loss:

○ you return to the same job with the same employer
○ you do a different job for the same employer
○ you undergo training for a different type of work
○ you look for a job with a different employer.

same job, same employer

If your disability is temporary, let your employer know about the nature of your injuries and the amount of time it is likely to be before you are fit to return to work. If you are in hospital, the hospital social worker may be prepared to do this for you. If your employer knows that you will be able to return to work in 3 months or 6 months or whenever, he may be able to arrange short-term cover for the job, thus preserving your employment.

If your disability does not affect the way in which you can perform your work, there is no reason why you should not return to the same job. It may, however, be necessary for some small changes to be made. A person whose back injury prevents him from operating a machine which is an essential part of his job, may still be able to use the machine if it is adapted in some way. It may, for instance, be possible to move switches so that they can be operated from a seated position.

It may be worth asking the DRO to liaise with your employer regarding your return to work and to ensure that your employer knows about ways in which the effects of your disability can be minimised.

The Manpower Services Commission can, where appropriate, purchase special or additional equipment needed, or pay for adaptations to enable a disabled person to perform his job.

different job, same employer
In some cases, it is impracticable to return to your previous job. Someone who has had a leg amputated, for example, may be unable to return to a job which involves a considerable amount of standing and walking.

Do not automatically resign. Find out whether there is a different job within the same company which you could undertake and whether the employers are willing to offer you alternative work. Your trade union representative or the DRO should be able to help.

It is often assumed that a person who is newly disabled must automatically take a job involving less strain or responsibility. There is, however, no reason why there should not be a sideways transfer or even promotion.

If the replacement job means less pay, this may be an element (loss of earnings) in your claim for damages.

being dismissed
Although you may eventually be able to perform the same job, your employer may be unable or unwilling to hold the job for you. A small company may not be able to keep the job open for a long period if there are insufficient staff or means to provide cover for that time. It could be that the employer's premises are unsuitable for somebody with your disability and do not lend

themselves to being adapted. Or the employer has a policy of dismissing people who are on sick leave for more than a certain period of time. Or he may not understand your disability and may want to get rid of you.

An employer may seek to dismiss you if your absence due to the injury is prolonged, but for the dismissal not to be 'unfair' under the employment legislation he will have to establish that you are now incapable of doing the work for which you were employed and that there are no suitable alternative jobs he can offer you. In other circumstances, you may have a claim for unfair dismissal and should seek advice on this.

training for different work
One assumption to avoid is that because you have never done a particular type of work in the past, you will be unable to do it now, when you have also to contend with a disability. There are, however, cases of manual workers who, after suffering a physical disability, have moved into the professions – for example, a miner who broke his back became a chartered accountant. Conversely, a salesman who was left deaf and dumb after an accident became a shepherd.

The Manpower Services Commission offers disabled people opportunities for training. Most courses are on ordinary training schemes at skillcentres or further education colleges, which are not specifically designed for disabled people. There are, however, four residential training colleges which cater specifically for disabled people. These provide courses in subjects such as computer programming, clerical and commercial subjects, watch and clock repair, mechanical engineering, electrical engineering, instrument making.

employment rehabilitation
If you are unsure of your abilities or the type of work it would be best for you to train for now, it could be worth attending an MSC employment rehabilitation centre (ERC) for occupational assessment and vocational guidance.

ERCs are attended mainly by people who have lost their job due to an injury or illness and have been out of work for some time, to help them regain confidence and working ability.

General information about ERCs is given in an MSC leaflet available at jobcentres, which includes a map showing the location of countrywide network of centres. In addition, there are a small number of ASSET (assistance towards employment) centres which also provide assessment, but offer work experience with employers rather than in the centres themselves.

Going on an ERC course will not teach you a trade but will enable you to try out different types of job, such as clerical and commercial work, bench engineering, machine operating, woodworking, outdoor work, and sedentary work such as packing and assembling. The intention is to discover what you can do best and what interests you most, and to give you confidence to do an ordinary job.

You will be credited with national insurance contributions throughout the course. DHSS leaflet NI 125 *Training for further employment*, available at unemployment benefit offices, explains how to protect your right to NI benefits if you are taking an approved course of full-time training.

At the end of the course, the ERC sends a confidential report on you to your local jobcentre, and may send a copy to your GP. Most employment rehabilitation centres also provide clients with a summary report for their own information.

The Health and Safety Executive has an employment medical advisory service (EMAS), which can give a confidential medical assessment, in many cases through an ERC, of the kind of work that might suit someone with your disability or health problem and what work should be avoided. Medical treatment is not given, and EMAS has no job-finding function but the medical advisers liaise with DROs at jobcentres. A leaflet listing the regional EMAS offices and the areas they cover is available from the Health and Safety Executive, St Hugh's House, Stanley Precinct, Bootle, Merseyside L20 3QY.

looking for a job

The charity **Opportunities for the disabled** provides an employment service, free for employers and jobseekers with disabilities. It is staffed by secondees from industry and commerce with the aim of ensuring that disabled jobseekers get a fair chance in the competitive field of open employment. There are twelve offices; the London address is 1 Bank Building, Princes Street, London EC2R 8EU (telephone 01-726 4963).

Always ask your friends whether there are any vacancies where they work. Current employees are often the first to learn of vacancies and many jobs are advertised internally before external advertising is considered. Your friend may also be able to put in a good word for you to get an interview.

Another obvious source is newspaper advertisements. For general jobs, local newspapers are probably as good as any, but for jobs in local government or central government, national newspapers can be better, with specific sections featured on particular days. Public reference libraries keep copies of newspapers and of many trade and professional magazines.

About 30 per cent of job vacancies are displayed at jobcentres. As well as a self-service section, most jobcentres have an employment adviser as well as a disablement resettlement officer, who can be asked for individual advice. Most of the jobs offered through jobcentres are skilled or semi-skilled.

There is a special MSC service for people of managerial or professional status, called Professinal Executive Recruitment (PER), which can be contacted through a jobcentre. PER and DROs are supposed to liaise to ensure that the most efficient service is provided to disabled people who are at managerial level or professionally qualified.

The **Association of Disabled Professionals,** which is run by disabled people, aims to improve the education, rehabilitation, training and employment opportunities for all disabled people. The ADP is not an employment agency and is unable to help directly with finding employment, but can help with advice and information on how to find and retain suitable employment. The address of the general secretary is The Stables, 73 Pound Road, Banstead, Surrey SM7 2HU.

registering as disabled

The Disabled Persons (Employment) Acts lay down that all employers who employ over 20 people should ensure that a proportion of their work force (a quota currently set at 3 per cent) is registered disabled. Only about a third of employers currently meet their quota of registered disabled employees. So it could increase your chances of getting a job if you are registered as disabled and would therefore add to the employer's statutory quota.

The Disabled Persons Register is a voluntary register kept by the Manpower Services Commission. You can apply to be registered if you are substantially handicapped in getting (or keeping) employment or working on your own account, and are likely to be so disabled for at least 12 months. You are expected actually to want some form of paid employment and to have a reasonable prospect of being, and remaining, employed.

You can apply through a jobcentre. You will need to produce medical evidence from your own doctor or the hospital (the jobcentre may obtain this if you are still an inpatient). There is a special form for your doctor to complete (he may charge you for this) or you may have to have a special medical examination arranged by the jobcentre.

Once registered, you get a certificate of registration which you can show a prospective employer so that he knows employing you will help him to fulfil his statutory duty.

Registration is granted for a specified period – anything from one year to ten years on until retirement age. You can apply to renew the registration if your handicap persists beyond the period of the certificate, or to have your name removed at any time.

fares to work scheme

Financial assistance can be given to registered disabled people who are unable to use public transport as a result of their disability and who, as a result, incur extra costs in getting to work. Assistance is given towards the cheapest reliable alternative to public transport, and the maximum amount payable is £65 a week. Leaflet DPL 13, available from a jobcentre, gives further details.

applying for jobs

Declaring your disability may restrict the number of job interviews you are offered. On the other hand, public employers, such as local authorities, are increasingly exercising positive discrimination towards disabled applicants. The civil service has departmental disabled persons' liaison officers whose function is to promote the employment of disabled people within that department. In such cases, declaring your disability may actually ensure that you are considered more seriously for an interview.

A recent study of discrimination in employment showed that people who did not declare their disability when applying for a job had a 1.6 greater chance of obtaining an interview than a person with similar background, experience and qualifications, who did declare a disability. Many disability organisations advise disabled people not to declare their disability until interview. In some cases, the disability is apparent – for instance, someone who uses a wheelchair or crutches or needs a stick. It is more problematic where the disability is not visible.

If you have not done so already, it would be wise when you reach the interview stage for a job to declare your disability. Otherwise, if you are taken on and the employer then discovers your disability, he may not be sympathetic to the fact, since you have misled him. You may even be held to be in breach of contract and subject to immediate dismissal.

Employment protection legislation provides employees with various rights against unfair dismissal. If you informed the employer about your disability before you were appointed and are later dismissed for reasons connected with your disability, the dismissal could be held to be unfair, whereas if the employer lacked knowledge of your disability, this could provide him with a basis for a fair dismissal.

Once you have made known your disability at the interview, you may need to put the interviewer at ease about the disability. It is probably a good idea to make it clear that you have no objection to discussing it with him.

A *Which?* report in March 1987 on the financial aspects of changing your job gives advice on what to look for and how to assess the value of an offered job, and provides useful information for any jobseeker, abled or disabled.

alternatives
There are alternatives to being a full-time employee. If you are in receipt of invalidity benefit from the DHSS, you are entitled to earn up to £26 a week 'therapeutic' earnings without losing any of the invalidity benefit. This applies only to work done under medical supervision, as part of your treatment or rehabilitation.

sheltered employment
If your disability is so severe that you would be unable to hold down a job in conventional employment but you are able to produce at least one-third of the output of an able-bodied person, you may qualify for 'sheltered' work.

Traditionally, sheltered employment for disabled people has been in sheltered workshops. Although most severely disabled people are still employed in these special workshops, an increasing number now get employment under the sheltered placement scheme, set up through the Manpower Services Commission. The scheme involves a sponsor to employ the disabled person and a host firm to provide the work and the workplace. The host firm pays the sponsor according to the disabled person's output, and the sponsor pays the disabled employee a set wage. The sponsor may be the local authority, a voluntary organisation or an established sheltered workshop. Some firms employ disabled people within their own organisation in a 'sheltered' capacity.

There is an MSC leaflet, *The sheltered placement scheme*, giving basic information, and further details can be obtained from the disablement resettlement officer at a jobcentre.

job sharing

If your disability is not so much a functional loss but a reduction in strength and energy so that you are capable of performing a job but not able to do it for the requisite number of hours on end, you might like to try job sharing.

This entails your finding another person equally suitable for the job and dividing the working time between you according to each's requirements. Your status is that of a full-time employee but you share the benefits of the job (pay, holidays, sick pay) with the other person in proportion to the time worked.

Sharing a job can only be done if the employer is in agreement. You can apply jointly with your sharer as a team or offer to fill a vacancy when you know an existing sharer is leaving. Sometimes it is possible to apply on your own as a potential job sharer and the employer could either match you with another applicant, or re-advertise the second half of the job if you are appointed.

Many employers, particularly local authorities, voluntary organisations and the civil service, have a job sharing policy now, as part of their equal opportunities programme.

An organisation providing information (but not jobs) about job sharing is **New Ways to Work** (309 Upper Street, London N1 2TY, telephone 01-226 4026). They give advice on job sharing needs; for Greater London, there is a computerised register to match partners seeking similar work. They also give advice about other flexible ways of working, such as reduced working hours agreements. Publications include *Job sharing: a guide for* *employees* (£1) and other pamphlets about rights and conditions.

working at home
In recent years, there has been an increase in the type of work that can be undertaken at home, in addition to the traditional 'outwork' such as assembling or making small items. The growth of information technology has made it possible to have a computer in your home and to use this to earn your living without having to go to an office.

Some ideas and possibilities for work that can be done at home are given in the Consumer Publication *Earning money at home*.

INDEX

OTHER
CONSUMER PUBLICATIONS

Avoiding heart trouble
Approaching retirement
Children, parents and the law
Divorce, legal procedures and financial facts
Earning money at home
The legal side of buying a house
Living with stress
Renting and letting
Starting your own business
Taking your own case to court or tribunal
Understanding cancer
What to do when someone dies
Which? way to buy, sell and move house
Wills and probate

Consumer Publications are available from Consumers' Association, Castlemead, Gascoyne Way, Hertford SG14 1LH and from booksellers.